The Birth of Di

Van der Plas Publications / Cycle Publishing

THE **BIRTH** OF **DIRT**

Origins of Mountain Biking

2nd, Updated and Expanded Edition

Frank J. Berto

With a contribution by **Charles Kelly**

Publisher's Information:

All trade and consumer inquiries to be directed to the publisher: Van der Plas Publications /
Cycle Publishing, http://www.cyclepublishing.com, 1282 7th Avenue, San Francisco, CA,
94122, USA. Tel.: (415) 665-8214; Fax: (415) 753-8572

Distributed by:

USA: Midpoint Trade Books
UK: Orca Book Services
Australia: Woodslane Pty.

Photo Credits:

Front cover photo: © Index Stock Photography
Back cover and frontispiece photos: © Wende Cragg
Other photos: Wende Cragg, Larry Cragg, Gary Fisher, Charles Kelly, Ed Koski, and others.

Publisher's Cataloging in Publication Data:

Berto, Frank J. The Birth of Dirt: Origins of Mountain Biking
Includes Index and annotated bibliography
128 p. 22.9 cm
Library of Congress Control Number 2008925814
ISBN 978-1-892495-61-7

Acknowledgments

My thanks to Joe Breeze, Gary Fisher, Charlie Kelly, Tom Ritchey, and Mike Sinyard for tape-recorded interviews. My special thanks to Charlie Kelly and Joe Breeze for letting me use their extensive files of early mountain bike history.

Thanks also to Alan Bonds, Tim DuPertuis, Ben Lawee, Russ Mahon, Erik Koski, Wende Cragg, and John Finley Scott for long telephone interviews.

There is a dearth of published mountain bike history prior to 1978. There are very few pictures of clunkers and riders for the period from 1972 through 1977. The information for this period is based on the recollections of the people who were part of the action. All of the participants reviewed drafts of this paper, made corrections, and suggested improvements.

I apologize for the poor quality of some of the illustrations. These were reproduced from old magazines and catalogs, and are simply not available in a form more suitable for reproduction.

Regarding this revised edition, I was pleased to have a second chance at *The Birth of Dirt*. It allowed me to tell how the development of the mountain bike in Marin in the 1970s totally changed the kind of bicycle that the world rides today.

Billy Savage's 2007 movie "Klunkerz" is a significant addition to the history of the mountain bike. Billy interviewed all of the "usual suspects," and in the process he unearthed a broader view of the Marin County events.

Savage used the first edition of *The Birth of Dirt* as the basis for his movie. I have added some new material from "Klunkerz" in this edition.

I also took the opportunity to read most of the articles on mountain bike history that have been written since 1999, and made corrections and additions. I have also added many new illustrations.

Thanks also to the many people who wrote to me with suggestions and comments.

Author's Preface

The inspiration for this book came from Joe Breeze's article, "Who Really Invented the Mountain Bike?" in the March 1996 issue of *Bicycling* magazine, and Gary Fisher's rebuttal in the next issue. I know both Joe and Gary well, and it wasn't clear to me who was right. I thought I'd take a couple of weeks, sort out the facts, and write a paper to present at the 1997 International Cycle History Conference.

I planned to interview the principal players, write a first draft, and let everyone review what I had written. Everyone would get at least two cracks at checking the accuracy of their account.

Well, it didn't turn out quite that way. The paper took three months and went through fifteen drafts. Every time I thought I had put an item to rest, new facts would turn up. I talked to Gary Fisher and Charlie Kelly half a dozen times each, and to Joe Breeze a dozen times.

After the paper was presented and published, my publisher suggested expanding the subject to create a book, including many more illustrations. Now 10 years later, after the first edition finally sold out, I got a second crack at it. I think it's now no longer necessary to ask or answer the question "who invented the mountain bike." So this edition of *The Birth of Dirt* has evolved into the history of mountain biking.

Publisher's Introduction

This book started out as a research paper to answer a specific question: "Who invented the mountain bike?"

After the original paper was presented at the 1997 International Cycling History Conference in Glasgow, Scotland, more facts emerged. Mountain bike pioneer Joe Breeze in particular took great pains to analyze every piece of information included in the first draft of the manuscript.

With all that material in hand, we asked the author to compile it all in the form of a book. That's what led to the first edition of *The Birth of Dirt*.

Since the first edition was published in 1998, another ten years have gone by, and here it is: a second edition that includes practically all the known facts about the subject. This book now truly is "The Definitive History of Mountain Biking."

Throughout the book, we have made grateful use of relevant period photographs by Wende Cragg and others, most of them mountain bike pioneers in their own right.

Our special thanks to Charlie Kelly, keeper of the sacred records, for agreeing to check the completed proofs for factual accuracy. Any remaining errors are of course the publisher's and author's responsibility.

Table of Contents

Introduction.
Impact of the Mountain Bike

Beginning around 1982, a wave of change rolled over the bicycle industry. It significantly changed the kind of bicycles that were sold in America and Europe. Soon after, the changes spread to the rest of the world.

Buyers and bicycle makers switched from road bikes to mountain bikes. Tires went from skinny to fat, and riders went from a crouched posi-

Left and above: Figs. 0.1 & 0.2. The introduction of the mountain bike (above) revolutionized the way Americans ride bicycles. The 10-speed road bike (left) rapidly lost ground to the mountain bike and its derivatives.

tion on dropped handlebars to a more erect position on flat handle-bars.

Simply put, the invention of the mountain bike changed the kind of bicycle that the world rides today.

There had been a similar change 100 years before: In the 1880s, the switch from "high" bicycles (also known as "ordinaries") to "safety" bicycles had the same kind of impact. The safety bicycle evolved by degrees and there was no true inventor. Many historians pick John Kemp Starley's 1885 Rover as the first true safety bicycle.

By 1983, all of the major bicycle makers were offering at least one mountain bike. By 1984, they had multiple models. Sales of mountain bikes in the U.S. rose exponentially —from 5,000 in 1982 to 50,000 in 1983 to 500,000 in 1984 to 5,000,000 in 1985. I can think of no other product in any industry that grew by an order of magnitude every year for four years.

Like the safety bicycle, the transition from road bikes to mountain bikes also took about four years, although small numbers of road bikes continued to be made.

Above: Fig. 0.3. A 1887 Coventry Machinist's Co. high bicycle.

Right: Fig. 0.4. Starley & Sutton's 1886 Rover was the definitive safety bicycle. The transition from the high bicycle to the safety bicycle took about four years, from 1886 to 1890.

In the process, the mountain bike became a "bicycle" and the traditional dropped-handlebar ten-speed from the 1970s became a "road bike." By 1993, road bikes had less than 5% of the U. S. market. The mountain bike was more reliable and easier to ride, and it attracted a whole new class of buyers.

The mountain bike transition started out with a couple of dozen pot-smoking hippies just having fun on the slopes of Mount Tamalpais in Marin County, California. Nobody started out thinking that they were going to change the bicycling world. It just worked out that way.

As time passed, a number of them became missionaries in what became a mountain bike crusade. I was an infidel back in the 1970s. I remember telling Gary Fisher that ten mountain bikes would saturate the market. That would be the total population of nut cases who would pay $500 for an old Schwinn with good brakes and derailleurs.

I didn't get it. The time was ripe for something better than skinny-tired ten-speeds with dropped handlebars. Almost by default, some of the hippies became mountain bicycle entrepreneurs and a few years later their success attracted the traditional bicycle makers

The success of the mountain bike opened the tradition-bound bicycle business to innovation and change. Bicycle makers and bicycle buyers began thinking "outside the box." The mountain bike lured technically smart people into the bicycle industry. The burst of innovation was similar to the 1880s. Today, bicycle buyers have the choice between several different flavors of user-friendly bicycles with wider tires and flat-handlebars:

Fig. 0.5. An example of an early (1977) mountain bike—from the days before they were called mountain bikes. This is one from the second batch of custom-built Breezers.

❑ Inexpensive "City" bikes with medium-width tires.

❑ Expensive "Transportation" bikes, which are city bikes with lights, fenders and luggage racks.

❑ "Comfort" bikes, which are beginner's bike with suspension seatposts and suspension forks for a very soft ride.

❑ "Hybrid" bikes which are designed for both on-road and off-road use.

There are also "Street" bikes, and "Trekking" bikes, but the definitions vary with the different makers. All of these bikes are more practical and more saleable than most of today's skinny-tired road bikes, which are good for racing, but not much else.

Over the decades since then, mountain bikes themselves have also evolved into different varieties for different users. Mountain bike racing has become very popular, and specialized racing models have been developed, some of which are depicted in the concluding chapter of tis book, on page 123:

❑ Downhill bikes, with about 8 inches of front and rear suspension travel for downhill racing.

❑ "All-Mountain" bikes, with about 5 inches of suspension travel for cross-country racing.

❑ "Hardtail" bikes, with only front suspension to minimize weight for cross-country racing on more level terrain.

❑ "Freeride" bikes, for awesome stunts on purpose-built tracks.

Terminology varies between makers, but racing mountain bikes are only a small part of today's market. The standard inexpensive bicycle sold in American bike shops is a 24- or 27-speed mountain bike with front suspension. Chinese factories churn them out by the boatload to retail at big-box stores for less than $100.00.

The mountain bike is not just an American phenomenon. This type of bicycle has also become popular in most European countries, and the technology developed for, and introduced on the mountain bike has changed the look and feel of many other types of recreational and transportation bicycles sold in those countries.

Chapter 1.
Inventing the Mountain Bike

The mountain bike as we know it today originated in Marin County, in northern California, in the mid-1970s. The pedal-operated bicycle (velocipede) originated in Paris in the 1860s. The two events have one thing in common: two decades after the first prototypes appeared, people were arguing about who invented them.

This book will describe the development of the mountain bike as I witnessed it first hand, and as it was confirmed to me in 1996 by the six major participants: Gary Fisher, Charlie Kelly, Joe Breeze, Tom Ritchey, Alan Bonds, and Mike Sinyard.

Gary Fisher had long claimed to be the inventor of the mountain bike. After reading this book, Gary agreed that he was not the inventor.

Gary's claim was always controversial. None of the other people who

Right: Fig. 1.1. Three of the major players in the creation of the mountain bike. Left to right: Charles Kelly, Gary Fisher, and Joe Breeze.

were present during the gestation and birth process agreed that Gary was the inventor.

There are many similarities between the Michaux's and Lallement's conflicting claims to have invented the velocipede and Gary Fisher's claim to have invented the mountain bike.

I have a huge advantage over the bicycle historians who are still arguing about Michaux versus Lallement. I was living in Marin County and writing for *Bicycling* magazine during the whole transition from road bikes to mountain bikes. I know all of the main characters. Almost everyone is still alive. This book records their recollections of the events. Perhaps by studying the 1970s events, we can reevaluate the 1860s events and make a better judgment on who really invented the velocipede more than a hundred years before.

Above and right: Figs. 1.2 and 1.3. Historical parallel: Both Pierre Lallement (above) and Ernest Michaux (right), with his father Pierre, claimed to have invented the crank-driven velocipede around 1860.

Chapter 2.
Cast of Characters

To get the story, I tape-recorded the interviews with Gary Fisher, Joe Breeze, Charlie Kelly, Tom Ritchey, and Mike Sinyard. I interviewed or had long telephone conversations with Otis Guy, Alan Bonds, Russ Mahon, John Finley Scott, Tim DuPertuis, and Erik Koski.

I sent preliminary drafts of my paper for the International Cycle History Conference to all of the participants for comments and corrections. Here are some notes about the people involved.

Gary Fisher.

Gary Fisher was born in 1950. He started bike racing at age 12 and be-

came a Category One racer. He was riding and building fat-tired

Right: Fig. 2.1. Gary Fisher for a long time claimed this bike was built in 1974. However, several of its components were not available until mid-1975, and even later.

clunkers from 1973 onward. He participated in eight Repack races and won four times, and he holds the record for the fastest time. He was the first person in Marin to put derailleurs on a fat-tire bike.

In 1979, Gary founded a company called MountainBikes, with Charlie Kelly as his partner. In 1983 he started his own company, Fisher MountainBikes.

Joe Breeze

Joe Breeze was born in 1953. He was a Category One bicycle racer, and he started building bicycle

Fig. 2.2. Joe Breeze coming down Repack on his Breezer No. 1.

frames in the early 1970s after taking a class taught by master frame builder Alfred Eisentrout.

He started riding fat-tire clunkers in Marin in 1973. He participated in 19 Repack races and won 10. In 1977 and 1978, he built ten frames and assembled ten purpose-built mountain bikes. These ten Breezers demonstrated that there was a market for all-new mountain bikes.

Charlie Kelly

Charlie Kelly was born in 1945. In the mid 1970s Charlie shared a house at 32 Humbolt Avenue in San Anselmo with Gary Fisher and Alan Bonds. Charlie raced in 10 Repack races. He and Gary Fisher founded MountainBikes in 1979.

Charlie was the writer, publicist and keeper of the sacred records of early mountain biking. In August 1980, Charlie launched *The Fat Tire Flyer*, the first periodical devoted to mountain biking. Old *Fat Tire Flyers* are the prime source of information on the early mountain bike era.

Tom Ritchey

Tom Ritchey was born in 1956. He was a successful Junior and later a Category One racer. He became a full-time bicycle frame builder as soon as he graduated from high school. In 1979, he built the first dozen frames for MountainBikes. He was a rapid and prolific frame builder noted for his flawless fillet brazing. From 1979 to 1982, Tom built about half of the frames for the first 2,000 mountain bikes.

Alan Bonds

In the 1970s Alan Bonds shared a house with Gary Fisher and Charlie

Kelly. He participated in 20 Repack races and won 4 times.

He sold old frames, repainted frames, and complete clunkers. He was the major source of clunker bikes in the early 1970s, keeping the critical mass growing.

In 1976 he bought a trove of about 100 old bikes from an Oregon bike mechanic referred to as Legendary Wocus. Alan refinished them, and sold many of them as single-speed or derailleur clunkers.

Mike Sinyard

Mike Sinyard was born in 1949. In 1979, while on vacation in Italy, he met the Cinelli family. This led to the founding of Specialized Bicycle Imports, which imported and sold

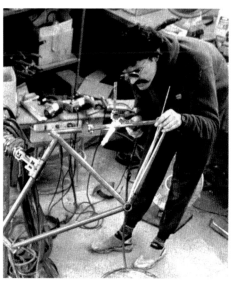

Above: Fig. 2.3. Charlie Kelly meticulously keeping records. It's a good thing he did, because many of his records form the basis for the information in this book.

Right: Fig. 2.4. Tom Ritchey brazing a frame in his workshop.

rare and exotic Italian bike parts. In 1982, Mike arranged for the Specialized Stumpjumper to be built in Japan. This was the first widely advertised, mass-produced mountain bike sold in regular bike stores.

Wende Cragg

Wende, the "Queen of Clunking," was an early mountain biker who

ran some very decent times down Repack—more than a minute faster than Frank Berto. She was one of the twelve finishers of the first ride from Crested Butte to Aspen over Pearl Pass. She also took most of the photographs that you see here and elsewhere of the early riders on Mount Tam and beyond.

Steve Potts

Steve was a member of Velo-Club Tamalpais (VCT). He raced on Repack. He was a frame builder and one of the founders of Wilderness Trail Bikes. In the early 1980s, he joined with Mark Slate and Charles Cunningham to form Wilderness Trail Bikes.

Above: Fig. 2.5. Alan Bonds coming down Repack on one of his derailleur clunkers.

Right: Fig. 2.6. Mike Sinyard flanked by some of his Specialized crew in the late 1970s

Mark Slate

Mark worked with Erik Koski on early mountain bikes. He was the third founding member of Wilderness Trail Bikes.

Charles Cunningham

Charles was a skinny-tire rider out on the trails, but later joined the mountain bike scene. In 1978 he made an aluminum-framed mountain bike for his own use. It weighed 24 pounds, considerably lighter than either Joe Breeze's or Tom Ritchey's early mountain bikes, and it attracted a small number of well-heeled buyers.

Otis Guy

Otis Guy was a Category One bike racer, who teamed up with Joe Breeze in 1977 to set the trans-America tandem record. He participated in 8 Repack races and won once. He was active during the formative 1974 to 1977 period. He

Above: Fig. 2.7. Wende Cragg, court photographer of, and participant in, the early years of mountain biking.

Left: Fig. 2.8. Three Wilderness Trail founders. From left to right, Charles Cunningham, Mark Slate, and Steve Potts.

was a firefighter and a part-time frame builder who made about 25 road and mountain bikes per year. He is now retired and lives in Fairfax.

Russ Mahon

Russ Mahon lived in Cupertino, south of San Francisco. He belonged to an early group of mountain bike riders who called themselves the Morrow Dirt Club. In 1973, he and his fellow club members built the first clunkers with derailleurs, and all of the other key mountain bike features. Gary Fisher saw Russ Mahon's derailleur clunker in December 1974.

John Finley Scott

John Finley Scott was a sociology professor at the University of California, Davis. In 1953, long before its time, he built a 9-speed fat-tire bike with hybrid gearing (3-sprocket freewheel plus 3-speed Sturmey Archer hub). In the 1960s he built a 10-speed "Woodsy Bike" with 650B rims and tires.

Above: Fig. 2.9. Otis Guy coming down Repack on a Breezer. He's using the cantilever brake to slide the rear wheel.

Right: Fig. 2.10. Russ Mahon clunkering near Cupertino, California.

In 1979 he bought 110 mountain bike frames from Tom Ritchey, and loaned $10,000 to Gary Fisher to help the MountainBikes startup. John provided funding at a critical time in the Marin mountain bike development.

After John retired from teaching, he was living alone in an isolated cabin with his double-decker bus parked on the same lot. He was murdered there in 2006. Although his body was never found, there was sufficient evidence to identify and convict the murderer in 2007.

Above: Fig. 2.11. John Finley Scott showing off his oversize TA chainring for his small-wheel Bike Friday, photographed the year before his death.

Right: Fig. 2.12 The Koski brothers in their parents' Cove Bike Shop in Tiburon, California.

Tim DuPertuis

Tim DuPertuis was born in 1952. He lived in Mill Valley and started racing road bikes while attending high school. He belonged to Velo-Club Tamalpais. He built a geared clunker in 1972 using an old Schwinn cantilever frame with 24 x 2.25 inch wheels. Two months later, he sold the bike for $50.00 to help finance his trip to Europe and disappeared from the fat-tire scene. Two years later, he came back and built another geared clunker. This bike had a Sturmey Archer 3-speed hub with drum brake.

Erik Koski

Erik Koski was born in 1952. He and his two younger brothers, Don and David, were working in their parents' Cove Bike Shop in Tiburon

in the mid-1970s. Their shop was a major supplier of the specialist components used in the early geared clunkers. Erik made and sold Trailmaster mountain bikes in 1980.

Fred Wolf

Fred Wolf worked with Charlie Kelly as a roadie for The Sons of Champlin rock band. He was a member of the Velo-Club Tamalpais, and together with Mark Vendetti, he introduced Gary Fisher, Joe Breeze, and Otis Guy to the fun of riding clunkers on the slopes of Mount Tam in the mid 1970s. Fred participated in 17 Repack races and won once.

Mark Vendetti

Mark was a member of the Larkspur Canyon Gang. He became a Category One road bike racer and belonged to Velo-Club Tamalpais. He spread the gospel of fat-tire riding to the other members of VCT.

Above: Fig. 2.13. Denise Caramagno, editor of *The Fat Tire Flyer* and a strong mountain biker herself.

Left: Fig. 2.14. Fred Wolf coming down Repack.

Craig Mitchell

Craig built the first custom-built mountain bike frame for Charlie Kelly in 1976, and Charlie feels that Craig should get a lot more credit than he did. He died in 1997.

Denise Caramagno

Denise was Charles Kelly's girlfriend. She took over as editor of *The Fat Tire Flyer*, at least nominally, from the third issue. She was an active mountain bike rider in her own right and made several runs down Repack.

Bob Burrowes

Bob was a West Marin firefighter who participated in 13 Repack races.

Mert Lawill

Mert was a motorcycle racer, who worked with Erik Koski to design and build the Lawill-Knight Procruiser mountain bikes.

Victor Vincente of America

Born Michael Hiltner, he changed his name to Victor Vincente of America (VVA for short) after setting the two-way trans-America record in 1975. He was a serious Southern California road racer before joining the mountain bike movement, riding in the second Crested Butte to Aspen tour. In 1979 he started building the Topanga mountain bike. In the 1980s he participated in, and promoted, numerous mountain bike races, tours, and "events" in Southern California.

Right: Fig. 2.15. Victor Vincent of America (VVA), one of the more colorful characters of early mountain biking, taking a break during the second Crested Butte to Aspen event.

Chapter 3.
The Mountain Bike Defined

Before claiming that XYZ invented the mountain bike, we must define what we mean by "mountain bike" and by "invent." Different definitions of those terms might result in a different inventor.

Frank Berto's Definition of "Mountain Bike"

In order to qualify as a mountain bike, the bike should satisfy the following six criteria, in order of importance:

❏ Tires at least 2 inches wide. All of the early bikes used knobby 2.125-inch wide tires.

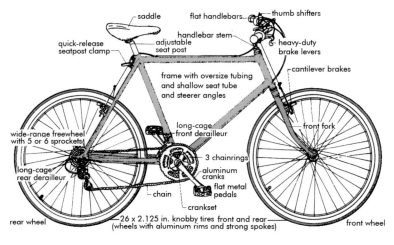

saddle — flat handlebars — thumb shifters
quick-release seatpost clamp — handlebar stem — adjustable seat post — heavy-duty brake levers
frame with oversize tubing and shallow seat tube and steerer angles — cantilever brakes
long-cage front derailleur — front fork
wide-range freewheel with 5 or 6 sprockets
long-cage rear derailleur — 3 chainrings — aluminum cranks — flat metal pedals
chain — crankset
rear wheel — 26 x 2.125 in. knobby tires front and rear (wheels with aluminum rims and strong spokes) — front wheel

Left: Fig. 3.1. This 1983 illustration shows the state-of-the-art mountain bike at the time. Although the brakes have changed and most now come with a suspension fork, it still defines the mountain bike today,

❑ Designed for off-road use. In the beginning, this meant that they had knobby tires, strong frames, high bottom brackets, long cranks, relaxed frame angles, and heavy duty, mud-proof components. Quick-release seatposts were often used so that the saddle could be lowered for descents.

❑ Derailleur gearing. The first Marin fat-tire bicycles were called "clunkers" (sometimes spelled "klunkers") or "ballooners." They used one-speed coaster brakes. (For the benefit of my British readers, "coaster brake" is the American term for what you know as a "backpedalling brake.")

By the time they were sold as mountain bikes, they had front and rear derailleurs, wide-range gearing with at least 15 speeds, three chainrings on the front, and five or six sprockets on the back. The lowest gear was 26 inches or less. Until about 1983, SunTour thumb-shifters mounted on the handlebars were a hallmark of mountain bikes.

❑ Good brakes. The early clunker bikes had ineffective coaster brakes. They needed better

brakes because they were developed on the slopes of Mount Tamalpais and many were used as downhill racers. The rear coaster brakes on the old clunkers could not dissipate much heat. One of the first clunker upgrades was the installation of drum brakes from old tandems or old Schwinns, if the rider could find them.

The first custom-built mountain bikes used cantilever brakes. Cantilevers worked well in dry conditions, but with the chrome-plated steel rims used in the early days, they did not stop well in the wet. Once aluminum rims became available, cantilever brakes were universally used. Brake levers, cables, and casings from motorcycles were used to optimize the effectiveness of the brakes.

❑ Flat, roadster-style handlebars. With some exceptions, a bike with dropped racing handlebars, isn't a mountain bike.

❑ Marin County, California, origin. This is not a technical feature but it defined which early bikes were part of the lineal development of today's mountain bikes. Just as the pedal-driven velocipede originated in Paris in the 1860s, so the mountain bike originated in Marin County in the 1970s.

Elsewhere, dozens of derailleur-geared fat-tire roadsters with good brakes had also been built before 1975—many more than I have listed. They were not mountain bikes, because nothing came of them.

Why These Six Criteria?

The above definition describes the first generation of mountain bikes from, say, 1977 to 1983. Except for the frame geometry, it's still a reasonable description of today's mountain bikes, including full-

Below: Fig. 3.2. Mt. Tamalpais, or "Mt. Tam," (shown here from a spot near San Quentin prison) is the dominant feature in Marin County.

suspension "motorless motorcycles" used for downhill racing.

Many of the principals who were involved in the development of the mountain bike seem to have a simpler definition. In their view, the installation of derailleur gearing on a fat-tired bicycle converted that bike to a mountain bike.

Definition of "Invent"

This is a more critical and more controversial issue, because the definition may well determine the inventor. There are several dictionary definitions for the verb "invent." The usage that applies to bicycles is the following one quoted from three common dictionaries:

❑ *Webster's Second International Dictionary* of 1954: "To discover as by study or experiment; produce for the first time; as to

invent printing. Synonyms: Invent, create, discover, means to bring into being something new. Invent always implies fabrication, now, especially as the result of study, experiment, etc. Create implies an evoking into being, originally out of nothing but, later, as if out of nothing. Discover presupposes the existence of something and lack of knowledge and therefore implies its finding by exploration, investigation, etc. One invents a device, creates a work of art, discovers the laws of motion."

❏ *Random House*: "To originate or create as a product of one's own ingenuity, experimentation or contrivance: to invent the telegraph."

❏ *Oxford*: "To find out in the way of original contrivance, to create, produce, or construct by original thought or ingenuity."

Right: Fig. 3.3. The invention of the square-wheeled bicycle by Frank Berto's definition. The inventor has the original idea, makes the first prototype, and is actively involved in the development of the invention.

Frank Berto's Interpretation

Based on the dictionary definitions, I believe that a genuine inventor must pass three tests:

❏ First, the inventor must have the original idea and not copy someone else's prior idea.

❏ Second, the inventor must make the first prototype, which cannot be a copy of someone else's prototype.

❏ Third, the inventor must actively participate in the subsequent developments that lead to the utilization of the invention. A genuine inventor must pass all three tests.

IDEA

PROTOTYPE

SQUARE² CORP.

PRODUCTION

Terminology Used in This Book.

I use the word "clunker" to describe a pre-mountain bike that had an old balloon-tired roadster frame. There were coaster-brake clunkers and derailleur clunkers. I use the term "mountain bike" to describe a bicycle with a brand new frame that sat-isfies the mountain bike definition. Everything before Joe Breeze's 1977 Breezer was a clunker. A "cruiser" is a single-speed, coaster brake, balloon-tired bicycle that was and still is popular in Southern California. A BMX bike is a single-speed bike used by teenagers for "Bicycle Moto-Cross" and trick riding.

Fat-tire bikes that aren't mountain bikes:

Top left: Fig. 3.4. Derailleur clunker, built up by Gary Fisher for Bob Burrowes.

Bottom left: Fig. 3.5. Cruiser (this is a modern replica of an early Schwinn cruiser).

Above: Fig. 3.6. BMX bike (a 20008 model).

Chapter 4.
Criteria for Invention of the Mountain Bike

Assuming that the mountain bike resulted from an invention rather than from evolution, then the inventor would have to meet the following criteria, roughly in order of importance:

❏ The inventor was first to conceive the idea for the mountain bike and he did not get the idea from someone else.

❏ The inventor made the first prototype mountain bike that included all of the definitive characteristics and that he did not copy someone else's earlier mountain bike. (If someone else's earlier mountain bike had all of the essential mountain bike characteristics, then that someone else could be the true inven-

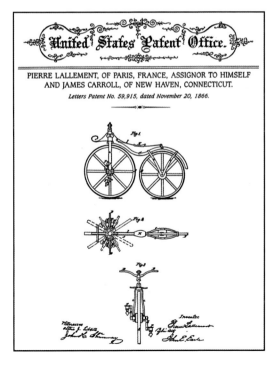

Right: Fig. 4.1. The first bicycle patent was issued to Pierre Lallement in 1866.

tor, if he met the rest of the requirements for inventor.)The inventor's prototype mountain bike was the "progenitor," i.e. the oldest ancestor of a direct line of bikes that became what we call mountain bikes today.

❑ The inventor was actively involved in the development of subsequent mountain bikes.

❑ The inventor was the first to use the name "mountain bike" to describe his bicycle.

❑ The inventor got a patent on the mountain bike. (Patents are good for dating ideas. However, the patent holder isn't always the inventor. He's just the first person to claim the invention at the patent office.)

The problems come when a device evolves over a period of time, rather than being one person's unique brainstorm. Somewhat similar devices usually existed prior to the "invention date." Someone always finds an earlier device that seems to disqualify any inventor.

Above: Fig. 4.2. Portrait engraving of R.W. Thompson, the first inventor of a pneumatic tire.

Left: Fig. 4.3. John B. Dunlop on a bike with his pneumatic tires. You can tell the two apart by the color of their beards.

That's why historians have so much fun debunking accepted history.

Comparison with the Invention of the Pneumatic Tire

The pneumatic bicycle tire is the classic example. Today, almost every bicycle history book states that John B. Dunlop invented the pneumatic tire in 1888. Yet, R.W. Thompson had previously patented the pneumatic tire in 1845 and Dunlop's patent should have been invalid because of what is called prior art in patent law.

Nevertheless, Dunlop meets the criteria for the inventor of the pneumatic tire, and it does not matter (to me anyway) whether Dunlop was aware of Thompson's previous invention. The thing that we call a tire today developed from Dunlop's 1888 efforts and not from Thompson's 1845 patent. Dunlop's tire was the progenitor of today's bicycle and automobile tires.

The mountain bike is defined by a combination of features and components. All of them had been invented earlier. It is easy to say (and probably true) that there is no true inventor because everything was prior art.

Alternatively, there may be an inventor who meets almost all of the criteria. In the chapters that follow, I present a chronology of the events that led to the mountain bike.

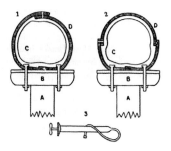

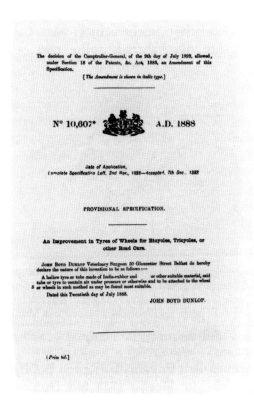

Above: Fig. 4.4. Patent drawing of Thompson's 1845 pneumatic tire patent.

Right: Fig. 4.5. Dunlop's pneumatic tire patent of 1888.

Chapter 5.
In the Beginning...

This and the three following chapters, will trace the developments from the earliest recognizable predecessors of the mountain bike up to the point when the term "mountain bike" had become accepted, around 1980.

1933: The Schwinn B-10E

Frank W. Schwinn, President of the Schwinn Company, introduced the Schwinn B-10E bicycle. This was the first mass-market bike in America since the 1890s to use wire-bead (clincher) tires with separate inner tubes. European bicycles had been using clincher tires with wire beads from the 1900s. American bicycle companies used horrid one-piece single-tube tires, basically garden hoses with valves. Their only virtue was their low price. Gresham's Law prevailed and the bad drove out the good.

Right: Fig. 5.1. Ignaz Schwinn, the founder of the Schwinn Company and the father of Frank W. Schwinn, who introduced balloon tire bicycles in the U.S.

34

Frank Schwinn was one manufacturer who rejected Gresham's Law. The B-10E used 26 x 2.125 inch low-pressure balloon clincher tires similar to the tires being used on cars (and on most bikes built in Europe at the time). Schwinn's balloon tire innovation created a new U.S. market for better quality bicycles.

The Excelsior was one of Schwinn's top quality bicycle models in the mid-1930s. The Schwinn Excelsior had the reputation of being the ideal frame for off-road downhill racing in Marin. It had a high bottom bracket so that the pedals cleared the rocks. Joe Breeze copied the Excelsior geometry in 1977. Tom Ritchey copied the Excelsior geometry in 1979 from Joe Breeze's Breezer. Mike Sinyard copied the Excelsior geometry in 1981 from

Arnold, Schwinn & Co.
Introduces
Super Balloon Tire Bicycles

LOW PRESSURE
18 to 22 Lbs.
According to weight of rider.

The only major development since the coaster brake—on the finest specially constructed bicycles built by the oldest and most outstanding American manufacturer. A 2¼" automobile type double-tube, straight-side, cord tire—on a new deep drop center rim—a construction embodying all the latest advancements in the tire art.

ARNOLD, SCHWINN & CO
1718 NORTH KILDARE AVE
CHICAGO.   ILLINOIS
TELEPHONE BELMONT 6793

MODEL B10E

Above: Fig 5.2. The B-1OE was typical of Schwinn's prewar balloon-tire bicycles. The basic frame geometry used shallow frame angles, lots of fork rake, and a high bottom bracket.

Top right: Fig. 5.3. Schwinn Motorbike. The Excelsior's frame geometry was similar.

Bottom right: Fig. 5.4. Joe Breeze's Schwinn Excelsior, which has a straight downtube, is in almost original condition.

Tom Ritchey's MountainBike. "Marin" geometry was standard on mountain bikes until about 1985.

In 1937, Schwinn introduced front and rear drum brakes. In the early 1950s, Schwinn introduced a strap-on cantilever front brake conversion kit. These rare items were much sought after by the early clunker builders.

1970–1971: The Larkspur Canyon Gang

Around 1970, precursors of mountain bikes appeared in Larkspur and Mill Valley, two small towns on the east slope of Mount Tamalpais in Marin County, just across the Golden Gate, north of San Francisco. The riders were in their teens and they called themselves the Larkspur Canyon Gang. Gang meant a group of friends rather than anything sinister.

John York, Mark Vendetti, Tom Slivka, Chris Lang, Otis Guy, Robert Kraft, Steve Potts and Robert Stewart were all members of the Larkspur Canyon Gang.

They started riding old one-speed coaster-brake newsboy bikes on the trails of Mount Tamalpais, just for kicks. They called their bikes "beaters" or "ballooners." In 1971,

Above: Fig. 5.5. A 1940 Schwinn Fore-Wheel drum brake would add much needed front-wheel braking to many early clunkers.

Right: Fig. 5.6. Material failure was not uncommon, as this bent fork testifies.

the Larkspur Canyon Gang ran a race from the top of Mount Tamalpais to Larkspur Canyon using any trail the rider chose. First prize was an envelope of pot. However, let it be said that, though a lot of marijuana was smoked in the early days of mountain bike development, not all of the riders were pot-smoking hippies.

At that time, technical innovation consisted of using the best coaster brake and fitting a front drum brake, if you could find one. If your bike broke, you threw it away and bought another one at the Goodwill Store for five dollars.

By 1974, the Gang had quietly disappeared, as the riders became more interested in cars and pickup trucks. Their key contribution was the members who had developed an enthusiasm for riding clunker bikes on Mount Tam. A bit later, they infected others in the Velo-Club Tamalpais with their enthusiasm.

1971: Velo-Club Tamalpais

Marin had a significant number of Category One, bicycle racers. However, many of them were part of the non-conformist, long hair, hippie, pot-smoking, counter culture that was prevalent in Marin at that time. They felt unwelcome in the Marin Cyclists, a more conventional racing club, so they formed Velo-Club Tamalpais, or VCT, their own "outlaw" club, in 1971. At it's peak, membership reached about 100.

Gary Fisher, Joe and Richard Breeze, Otis Guy, Charlie Kelly, Steve Wilde, Fred Wolf, Tim DuPertuis, Chris Lang, and Marc Vendetti, all raced for Velo-Club Tamalpais.

1973: The Spread of Clunkers

Marc Vendetti and Fred Wolf introduced off-road clunker riding to the Velo-Club Tamalpais. Marc rode his clunker to the club's monthly meetings. It didn't make sense to ride an expensive Italian racing bike at night. Marc persuaded other club members to go "clunking" on Mount Tam in the afternoon after a hard morning of road training.

Fig. 5.7. The Velo-Club Tamalpais emblem. Many of the VCT members joined the mountain biking crowd.

Joe Breeze, Otis Guy, and Charlie Kelly were early converts. They bought old clunker bikes and started riding them on the trails of Mount Tamalpais for training and for fun. Gary Fisher had been riding clunkers on and off since 1971.

By the end of 1973, there were 20 or 30 clunker riders in Marin, mostly men in their late teens and twenties. In the early 1970s, Marin's clunkers and their riders had a counter-culture image, especially to "straights" like your author, who had three teenage sons at the time. Most of the riders lived in Fairfax

and San Anselmo, two small towns on the north slope of Mount Tamalpais.

You didn't have to be a bike racer to ride a clunker in Marin. Firemen, bike shop mechanics, high school and college students were early riders, but after a while, just plain members of the general public bought clunkers and used them both on the trails and for general transportation.

Velo-Club Tamalpais provided the transition to clunker riding on Mount Tam from the Larkspur Canyon Gang. It provided the critical mass of young fit mountain bike riders. The early bikes were called many names, but in Fairfax and San Anselmo they were usually called "clunkers."

Upgrading the Clunker

Clunkers became more reliable as the riders learned that pre-war

Above: Fig. 5.8. The Morrow coaster brake could dissipate more heat and held up better on long down hills than other coaster bakes.

Right: Fig. 5.9. The Atom tandem drum brake that Gary Fisher's installed on his clunker.

Schwinn bike frames were best for severe use. They held up better than other brands, and they were also better than the newer Schwinn middleweight bicycles with their "cantilever" frames. They learned that Morrow and Musselman coaster brakes dissipated heat better than Bendix coaster brakes, which, in turn, were better than New Departure coaster brakes.

Front wheel brakes from any source were desirable. The lever-operated two-speed Bendix coaster-brake hub had a following. Long Ashtabula (one-piece) cranks were much sought after. Sturmey-Archer three-speed hubs fitted with large sprockets quickly "cratered" in clunker service with strong riders. Sturmey-Archer hub brakes over-

heated on long down grades. In a low key trial-and-error fashion, Marin's clunker riders improved the performance of their off-road bikes. There were no secrets. Improvements quickly became common knowledge.

Carlisle (Uniroyal) made knobby blackwall tires in 26 x 1.75 inch and 26 x 2.125 inch sizes. Parts were readily available. Schwinn, Huffy, AMF, Ross, and Roadmaster were still making "middleweight" coaster-brake one-speed bicycles with 26 x 1.75 inch tires that sold for $40 to $80. The Marin riders saved their money. They bought older, stronger bikes with wider 26 x 2.125 inch balloon tires at secondhand stores for $5.00 or so.

Marin County was fortunate in having a small number of bike stores that would order and stock the exotic parts for the growing clunker cottage industry.

Above and right: Figs. 5.10 and 5.11. Comparison of Schwinn frames: Pre-war B10-E (above) versus post-war "cantilever" design (right). The latter did not hold up as well as the pre-war design.

1972–1973: The Morrow Dirt Club

Independently from the Marin developments, a similar fat-tire movement took place in Santa Clara County south of San Francisco. Russ Mahon and his friends started riding old coaster-brake fat-tire bikes on the trails and fire roads in the Santa Cruz Mountains in the Cupertino area west of San Jose. They formed the Morrow Dirt Club, which grew to ten members. The club was

named after the Morrow coaster brake. Each member built his own off-road bike, which they called "bombers."

At the time, Russ Mahon worked as a carpenter. In his spare rime, he assembled three bomber bikes for his family and friends.

Other members included Bernie and Kathy Mahon, Tom and Carter Cox, Steve Mallet, Bill Hannat, Joe Pratters, Greg True, and Tom Secrest. The process of survival of the fittest old bikes set in. They determined that Morrow coaster brakes were better than Bendix or New Departure, hence the name of their club.

In February 1973, Russ built a rear wheel using a French Atom drum-brake hub and a five-sprocket freewheel. He installed this wheel on his Wards Hawthorne bomber bike. It already had a front drum

Above: Fig. 5.12. Russ Mahon's derailleur-geared "bomber" bike.

Right: Fig. 5.13. Members of the Cupertino-based Morrow Dirt Club with their clunkers—with and without derailleur gearing.

brake. He completed the bike with long-arm plastic brake levers, a Shimano Tourney rear derailleur, a double-chainring crankset, a front derailleur from a Schwinn Varsity, and SunTour thumb-shifters. Russ Mahon's February 1973 bomber bike met all of the technical requirements for a mountain bike—except for heavy-duty brake levers, cables, and casings.

By the end of 1973, about half of the members of the Morrow Dirt Club had abandoned coaster brakes and were riding ten-speed derailleur clunkers at a time when the Marin County riders were still using coaster-brake one-speeds. Their derailleur bomber bicycles were technically about two years ahead of those used in Marin. Russ made about six similar bikes for his friends.

The Morrow Dirt Club disappeared as the members got older and lost interest. We can only speculate why the mountain bike chain reaction took off in Marin County at the same time that it died out in the San Francisco Peninsula area.

Nobody in Marin remembered the names of the Morrow Dirt Club members. Decades later, Tom Ritchey heard about a Cupertino plasterer who had been mountain biking in the 1970s. Tom tracked him down, and it turned out to be Russ Mahon. It is Tom's account that allowed the story of the Morrow Dirt Club to be told here.

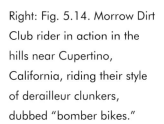

Right: Fig. 5.14. Morrow Dirt Club rider in action in the hills near Cupertino, California, riding their style of derailleur clunkers, dubbed "bomber bikes."

Chapter 6.
The Critical Years

Nineteen-seventy-four was the last year of the ten-speed bike boom in the U.S. and the year of the great gasoline shortage. It was the critical year for the invention of the mountain bike in Marin County.

The December, 1974 Mill Valley Cyclo-Cross Race

There's no question that on December 1, 1974, Russ Mahon, Bernie Mahon, and Carter Cox drove up from Cupertino to ride in the Mill Valley cyclo-cross race. They brought their three fat-tire derailleur clunkers. Each bike was a bit different, but all had drum brakes, front and rear derailleurs, and SunTour

Right: Fig. 6.1. Getting inspiration. Gary Fisher (left, in blue jersey) looking back to check out the derailleur gearing on the Cupertino riders' fat-tire bikes (foreground) at the start of the December 1974 Mill Valley cyclo-cross race. Years later Gary would claim that he had equipped his clunker with derailleurs before that time, and was merely looking at them because he did not think their brakes were adequate.

thumb shifters. At the end of the race, the three visitors took their bikes hack to Cupertino and dropped out of the mountain bike story.

Gary Fisher and Otis Guy both participated in this race. Gary rode his cyclo-cross bike. Charlie Kelly and Joe Breeze were spectators. Everyone saw the Cupertino bikes. The light bulbs flashed. Why not put derailleurs on a clunker so you could pedal up the hills? Within months, the first derailleur clunkers were riding the trails of Mount Tam.

Gary Fisher certainly saw the Cupertino bikes in the lineup. Charlie Kelly and Otis Guy believe that Gary Fisher got the idea of adding derailleurs and thumb-shifters to his clunker when he saw the Cupertino bikes. Gary Fisher's recollection is that he already had installed derailleurs on his clunker at that time. He was just surprised to see that somebody else was also building derailleur-geared clunkers, and that he thought they needed better brakes.

Gary Fisher's First Geared Clunker

Based on Gary Fisher's recollection, he built the first clunker with a Maxicar drum brake rear hub and a rear derailleur in September, 1974. Over the next few months, he added handlebar-mounted shift levers, a front derailleur, and a double-chainring crankset to this bike. The next year, he added a TA triple crankset and SunTour thumb-shifters. The pads on the Maxicar rear hub wore out, and Gary rebuilt the wheel using an Excelto rear hub.

Right: Fig. 6.2. Gary Fisher (on a conventional cyclo-cross bike, left) and Russ Mahon (on his derailleur geared "bomber" bike, right) in action at the December 1974 Mill Valley cyclo-cross race.

This is the Gospel according to Gary, but there are no pictures, nor other hard evidence, nor witnesses to support his claimed September 1974 date for this prototype bike. He had the prototype bike until 1996, and the bike is now in the Shimano Museum in Osaka, Japan. I saw it and photographed it in 1996, before it was shipped to Japan.

Prototypes outlive inventors, creating huge problems for historians. After fifty years or so, no experts are left to point out the anachronisms. There are good reasons for this problem. The inventor usually improves and upgrades the first prototype, destroying the original in the process.

The Mark 3 clunker that Gary showed me in 1996 was obviously assembled significantly later. It has major problems with a September 1974 production date because:

- ❏ The Cook Brothers BMX-style front fork was not available for 26-inch wheels until 1977. Pictures of Gary's 1975 and 1976 bikes show Ashtabula-style front forks (with the two blades forged together out of a U-shaped piece of steel.)

- ❏ The adapter that allowed a cotterless crankset (TA or any other) to be installed in a 2 inch diameter Ashtabula bottom bracket was not made until 1976 at the earliest. Gary could have used a double-chainring Ashtabula-style crankset in 1974, nor even in 1975, but not a cotterless TA triple.

- ❏ The Shimano 600 rear derailleur was not available until mid-1975. It was first advertised in the March 1975 *Bicycling* magazine as "New." I wrote a derailleur test article for that

Left: Fig. 6.3. This presumed "prototype" was probably Gary Fisher's Mark 3 derailleur clunker first assembled in 1975. Judging by the components, it is obvious that this bike could not have been assembled as shown here before 1977.

same issue, and I couldn't get a Shimano 600 to test yet.

Charlie Kelly and Otis Guy, who rode with Gary, recall that his first derailleur bike was a red and ivory B.F. Goodrich (made by Schwinn), and that it had stem-shifters mounted on the handlebars. The 1975 prototype has a nickel-plated Schwinn Excelsior frame and SunTour thumb-shifters. It first appeared after the summer of 1975. Joe Breeze is uncertain of the date, but he also recalls that Gary's first derailleur bike didn't have SunTour thumb-shifters. It had stem-shifters mounted on the handlebars.

Gary recalls that he built two or three more ten-speed clunkers in 1975, and there are undated pictures of two of them. Gary says that he built a clunker for Fred Wolf in 1975 with an Ashtabula double crankset and SunTour front and rear derailleurs. A Wende Cragg detail photo of this mud-covered bike is pictured in the September 1979 issue of *Mariah Outside* magazine (the same detail is featured on the half-title page of this book, i.e. the first

page, while Fred is shown with that bike below).

Charlie Kelly and Otis Guy agree that Gary assembled the first derailleur clunker with 26-inch wheels in Marin County. Viewed with hindsight, it's surprising that it took so long for the Marin pioneers to fit derailleurs to their clunkers. We aren't talking about rocket science. Almost all of the early riders worked on their own bikes and many were bike shop mechanics. Derailleurs were common in the bike trade during the 1970s.

When Gary and I reviewed the final draft of this paper together, he consented that the bike in the Shimano Museum was not built in 1974. Instead, he said, it was a rep-

Right: Fig. 6.4. Fred Wolf and his 1975 Fisher-built derailleur clunker. This was probably Gary Fisher's Mark 2 derailleur clunker.

lica, or reconstruction, of the "various clunkers" that he rode in the 1970s.

Bicycling! magazine (with an exclamation mark, which was part of the title at the time) played a small role in the mountain bike story. In the mid-1970s, *Bicycling!* was published in San Rafael, Marin County, California. It was a funky low-key

Above: Fig. 6.5. This is probably Gary Fisher's first derailleur clunker, almost certainly built in 1975. Note the Ashtabula forks and the Shimano Positron shift levers with two cables.

Right: Fig. 6.6. Road test article by Gary Fisher and Frank Berto in the April 1977 issue of *Bicycling!*

operation. Gary Fisher was their part-time road test rider, and I was a part-time technical writer.

We formed the road test team for *Bicycling!* We compensated for each other's strengths and weaknesses. Gary could feel subtle differences between various bicycles. I could write. This was my introduction to the mountain bike scene, which was happening a few miles from my home. My minor contribution was recommending the Huret Duopar to Gary for the later production bikes. This was my favorite rear derailleur at that time.

1975–1976: The Spread of Derailleur Clunkers

The derailleur clunker chain reaction went critical in 1975. Derailleur gearing improved the clunker's off-road capabilities. By the end of 1975, half a dozen people besides

Road Test: $180 to $205 – What Can You Get?

by Gary Fisher and Frank Berto

This road test is a first for *Bicycling!* Magazine, a test featuring several different brands of bicycles in one price range. We will be continuing with six more bikes next month: Windsor Super Carrera, Panasonic CX2000, Sentinel, Takara Grand Touring, Fuji 12-speed and the Peugeot Super UO-10.

Why $180 to $210? This is often the range a person chooses for his second bicycle. He's outgrown his beginner bike and is ready to try something a little more lively. Bicycle value

hooded brake levers on the Miyata to the safety levers on the other bicycles, and we appreciated the longer lever travel they afforded.

Derailleurs: The first place that Japanese component challenged the Europeans was in the derailleur department. Call that a rout. Consider the Sun Tour Cyclone. It's almost as jewel-like as the Huret Jubilee and at half the price. Other test bikes were equipped with the Sun Tour VGT and the Shimano 600 models. All are easily capable of handling the wide range gearing found on our five test bikes. Only lately have the Europeans been redesigning their derailleurs to meet

Gary Fisher had fitted derailleur gearing to their clunkers. Joe Breeze and Otis Guy stuck with their authentic single-speed coaster-brake clunkers. The number of Marin clunker riders grew to perhaps fifty.

The derailleur-equipped clunker slowly caught on. Some people built their own clunkers but a tiny cottage industry developed to convert old roadster bikes, mostly Schwinns, into clunkers and sell them.

Gary Fisher, Charlie Kelly, and Alan Bonds shared a rented house at 32 Humboldt Avenue in San Anselmo. They built clunkers for their own use and to sell to friends. Charlie sought out frames and components in his travels as a "roadie" with the Sons of Champlin rock band. Gary worked in the Wheels Unlimited bike store in San Rafael, and he knew where to find new components. Alan knew how to turn a rusty old frame into a nicely painted one.

Alan, Gary, and Charlie were not alone. By 1976, half a dozen other people were assembling derailleur clunkers in Marin.

1976: The "Legendary Wocus" Story

Robert Stewart had discovered a cache of old clunker bikes in the Wocus area of Oregon, near Klamath Falls. He told Alan Bonds about it, and in the summer of 1976 Alan Bonds and Ian Stewart (Robert's brother) drove a truck to Klamath Falls to check it out. They asked for directions to the Wocus Bike Shop at a gas station. "You mean Legendary Wocus," the man replied, and gave them exact directions.

Right: Fig. 6.7. A beautifully painted early derailleur conversion by Alan Bonds.

It wasn't a fantasy. The owner of the shop repaired bikes for the local kids. He had a house with a large lot, and he had been dismantling old bikes for many years. There were six huge piles of rusty bike frames in his back yard. Each pile was approximately thirty feet long by six feet wide. He had separate piles of wheels, forks, and handlebars. The hubs, brakes, chains, and other components were in pails and barrels in the outbuildings.

They made a deal to buy 50 frames complete with components for $3 dollars each. They were allowed to pick through the piles and barrels and select the choice items. They rooted through the piles for the rest of the afternoon until they filled the truck.

Alan and Robert went back a month later and bought another 50 bikes. Those two truckloads pretty much high-graded the Schwinn Excelsior frames, Morrow coaster brakes, Union drum brakes, and

other parts from the Legendary Wocus mother lode. Marin builders made pilgrimages to Klamath Falls for another five years to pick through the remnants.

Alan and the Stewart brothers now had a stockpile. They sandblasted frames, repainted them in authentic period colors, and assembled clunkers for the local Marin market. Alan's recollection is that he assembled about 25 clunkers in 1976. Most of them had derailleurs and drum brakes. Gary Fisher supplied Alan with the necessary special components. Alan recalls that Gary built about three clunkers, and Charlie Kelly built one clunker in 1976. Most of the other clunker assemblers bought frames from Alan. The Legendary Wocus trove helped the Marin mountain bike movement reach critical mass.

Faber's Schwinn Bike Shop in San Jose also had a back lot with a huge pile of old junk bikes. A number of early Marin builders, including Gary Fisher and the Koski brothers, drove down to Faber's and picked out the choice items. Erik Koski recalls buying as many as 50 clunker frames from Faber's.

Left: Fig. 6.8. Another derailleur clunker built up by Alan Bonds, this one leaning against a "portagee gate" on Mt. Barnaby, photographed by Charlie Kelly.

Derailleur Clunker Upgrades

Several bike shops in Marin started stocking "upgrade" components for derailleur clunkers. The Cove Bike Shop in Tiburon, Sunshine Bicycle Works in Fairfax, and Wheels Unlimited in San Rafael catered to Marin's road racers. As the clunker trade grew, these three stores began to stock SunTour thumb-shifters, Huret Duopar derailleurs, TA cranksets, Mafac cantilever brakes, Magura moto-cross or moped brake levers, and so on. The availability of these parts made it easier for the early pioneers to build and modify their clunkers.

By the end of 1976, there were as many as 100 derailleur-clunkers in Marin. At a time when a Campagnolo Record-equipped Schwinn Paramount cost $600, the going price for a clunker with derailleur gearing was around $400.

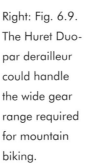

Right: Fig. 6.9. The Huret Duopar derailleur could handle the wide gear range required for mountain biking.

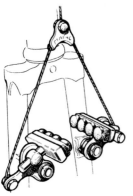

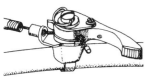

Left: Figs. 6.10–6.12. From top to bottom: Magura moto-cross brake levers, early thumb-shifter, and Mafac cantilever brake.

Bottom right: Fig. 6.13. TA triple chainrings and Simplex front derailleur.

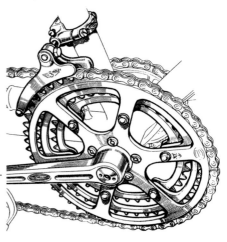

Chapter 7.
The Repack Races

The Repack race was a downhill time-trial held on the Pine Mountain fire road on Mount Tamalpais. The first race was on October 21, 1976. It was organized by Charlie Kelly and Fred Wolf to settle an argument over who was the fastest descender.

It was named Repack because the steep 2.1-mile (3.4 km) downhill course burned the grease out of the coaster brakes, and consequently the hub had to be taken apart and "repacked" (with fresh grease) before the next race. Seven people participated in the first race. Alan Bonds won. He was the only rider

Below: Fig. 7.1. Jerry Riboli's widely published photo of the lineup at the start of the 1976 Repack race. Counting from left to right: 1st is Fred Wolf; 2nd is Wende Cragg; 5th is Chris Lang; 8th is Charlie Kelly; 9th is Gary Fisher; 10th is Joe Breeze; 12th is Craig Mitchell; 15th is Alan Bonds. Ten of the riders had installed a front drum brake.

who didn't fall. There was a gate halfway down the course, which was closed and locked during the first race. Alan had practiced sliding under the gate. In subsequent races the gate was open.

Not everyone knew about the first race, so a second race was held a week later with a field of nine. Bob Burrowes won the second race on a 1950 Schwinn Spitfire rebuilt by Gary Fisher to include drum brakes and front and rear derailleurs.

Nine Repack races were held in 1976, eight in 1977, three in 1978, and two in 1979. There were "final" races in 1983 and 1984, a "Repack Reunion" on the 20th anniversary in 1996, and another one in 1997. I

Above: Fig. 7.2. Gary Fisher coming down Repack. This is the classic recovery position from a three-point turn.

Left: Fig. 7.3. D.S. Livingston's Repack course map of 1984 was based on Joe Breeze's course survey.

51

rode in the 1983 race, and my account is included in this book (see Chapter 19. Charlie Kelly's account of the 1996 Repack Reunion can be found in Chapter 20.

Charlie Kelly organized and publicized most of the Repack races, and he was the timer and record keeper. The scheduling depended on Charlie's travels with the rock band. Most of the races were held in the fall, after the end of the bicycle road racing season and after the first rains made the fire road more useable.

Gary Fisher won four races and set the course record of 4 minutes, 22 seconds, which still stands. Joe Breeze won the most races (10), and he holds the second-fastest time of 4 minutes, 24 seconds.

The Repack races were critical for the development of the mountain bike in Marin County. In a typical race, five or six racers would fail to finish because of mechanical failures. Winning depended largely on

Above: Fig. 7.4. Except for Alan Bonds, everybody took a spill along the course of the first Repack race.

Right: Fig. 7.5. It's 1979 and Repack organizer and time-keeper Charlie Kelly is being interviewed by Steve Fox of KPIX TV. Looking on are Tom Ritchey (far right) and his wife, Kathy. It provided the first "mainstream" exposure for mountain biking.

rider skill, but everyone sought to gain a technical edge. When something worked, it was quickly copied.

Joe Breeze and Otis Guy continued to ride their one-speeds, but it soon appeared that there was an advantage to derailleur gearing. Without the Repack proving ground, the mountain bike would probably have

Right: Fig. 7.6. Dust gets in your eyes. Fred Wolf prevents it by wearing goggles. Like most of the Repack photos you'll see, this shot was taken at "Camera Corner," because that's where the action looks most dramatic (and where most of the spills take place...)

Below: Fig. 7.7. At the top of the course. Everyone's getting ready for the descent. On the right is Wende Cragg, adjusting her camera.

developed differently, and it certainly would have taken longer.

Repack can be considered the American equivalent of the "Polymultiplié" touring bike trials and exhibitions that were held in Chanteloup, France, in the 1950s. These events contributed much to the development of bicycle components such as gears and brakes, just like the Repack races helped the Marin builders and riders determine what worked and what didn't in the way of frames and components.

Above: Fig. 7.8. Charlie Kelly scrubbing off speed in the November 1977 Repack race.

Left: Fig. 7.9. Fireman Bob Burrowes goes down in flames at Camera Corner in the December 1976 Repack race.

Below: Fig. 7.10. Summary of results, tabulated by Joe Breeze.

Racers	Repak Race #	Best Time	1st	2nd	3rd	4th	5th	#Repaks Entered
1) Gary Fisher	7	4:22.14	4	1	1	1	0	8
2) Joe Breeze	9	4:24.07	10	7	1	0	1	19
3) Otis Guy	8	4:25.08	1	2	0	3	2	8
4) Jimmy Deaton	24	4:34.20	2	0	0	0	0	2
5) Fred Wolf	15	4:35.60	1	6	3	1	2	17
6) Bob Burrowes	19	4:35.74	2	2	2	1	1	13
7) Craig Weichel	21	4:37.18	0	0	1	0	0	2
8) Alan Bonds	11	4:39.00	4	2	2	7	3	20
9) Erik Westerhoff	24	4:39.50	0	1	0	0	0	1
10) Joey Peterson	24	4:40.70	0	0	1	0	0	1
11) George Newman	6	4:44.58	1	1	1	1	1	5
12) Roy Rivers	19	4:44.79	0	0	0	1	1	5
13) Mike Jordan	23	4:45.88	0	0	1	0	0	1
14) Charlie Kelly	15	4:49.33	0	0	2	0	2	10
15) Noel Agajan	22	4:50.50	0	0	1	0	0	2

(Some rows add up to more than 24 due to ties.)

Chapter 8.
Purpose-Built Mountain Bikes

By 1976, more than a hundred people in Marin were riding clunkers. The troves of old frames within 100 miles from the San Francisco Bay Area, and as far north as the Oregon border area, were mined out.

There was a shortage of suitable frames to replace the casualties and to satisfy the new customers. There were plenty of newer middleweight Schwinn cantilever frames, but they didn't hold up as well as the older Schwinns.

The First Custom-Built Frame

Charlie Kelly weighed 180 pounds and was hard on bikes. In 1976, he asked Joe Breeze to build a custom

Right: Fig. 8.1. The first purpose-built mountain bike ever: Charlie Kelly on the bike Craig Mitchell built for him. Although it didn't handle well with the long-rake fork, its geometry was close to that of today's mountain bikes

clunker frame. Joe Breeze was busy, so Charlie asked Craig Mitchell, another local frame builder and Repack rider, to build a custom frame. Craig completed the frame in ten days. Rather than copying the Schwinn Excelsior frame dimensions, he provided steeper frame angles and a shorter wheelbase. Craig's first custom clunker frame was closer to the geometry of today's mountain bikes.

Charlie assembled the bike as a ten-speed with front and rear derailleurs. He fitted a set of Ashtabula forks that had too much rake for the frame's head tube angle. Consequently the bike handled poorly in downhill racing. Charlie dismantled it after two weeks and returned the frame to Craig. This was the first custom-built mountain bike. The frame was resold and reportedly shipped to Australia.

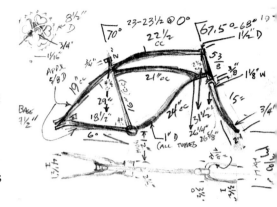

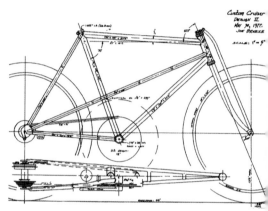

Left: Fig. 8.2. Design basis: Original Schwinn Excelsior conversion ridden by Alan Bonds.

Above: Fig. 8.3, 8.4 & 8.5. Three stages of design and development of the first Joe Breeze-built mountain bike frames of 1977.

The First Breezers

In the spring of 1977, Charlie Kelly again asked Joe Breeze to build him a clunker frame. Joe agreed and Charlie made a down payment. Joe was a good choice. He was an experienced frame builder and a good designer and machinist, in addition to being a road racer and a Repack clunker racer.

Above: Fig. 8.6. As happy as a kid at Christmas: Charlie Kelly with his new Breeze-built bike.

Left: Figs. 8.7, 8.8, & 8.9. Joe Breeze at work in his father's workshop, working on his first Breezer frame.

The frames of the Schwinn-based clunkers were weak and heavy. Some of the Schwinn clunkers weighed as much as 50 pounds. Joe designed a clunker frame that was both stronger and lighter. There was a significant local demand for custom-built mountain bikes and when the word got out, Joe got nine more orders.

He was a slow and methodical designer and builder. He prepared drawings and ordered tubing and components. The prototype, which was Joe's personal bike, was completed in September 1977. It was painted, and it had a handmade fork with fork braces. The other nine bikes were nickel-plated and used Cook Brothers BMX-style forks.

More Breezers

Joe Breeze kept going until he completed the remaining nine frames and they were assembled and delivered starting in June 1978. Everyone called them "Breezers."

The Breezer geometry was copied from the Schwinn Excelsior. On the basis of those dimensions, Joe designed a conventional diamond frame, using straight tubes with "twin-laterals," an pair of small-diameter tubes extending from the rear dropout to the head tube. The frame was made with straight-gauge chrome-moly aircraft tubing. The first Breezers weighed 38 pounds. Much of the weight was in the steel rims and heavy tires, but that was all that was available in 1978.

The Breezers were genuine mountain bikes, even though that

Above: Fig. 8.10. The first Breezer built in 1977, which became Joe's personal bike, had SunTour front and rear derailleurs and a TA triple crankset.

Left: Fig. 8.11. The second batch of Breezer frames ready to be painted and assembled.

name wasn't used at that time. They had Phil Wood hubs and bottom brackets, Dia-Compe cantilever brakes, Magura moto-cross brake levers, TA Cyclotouriste double or triple chainring cranksets, SunTour thumb-shifters, and either Shimano or SunTour derailleurs.

Thus, Joe Breeze designed and built the first modern mountain bikes. Breezers were new bicycles with all new components. They were widely seen and admired, and they proved that there was a market for something better than repainted old Schwinns. The Breezers expanded the market beyond Marin County. Gary Fisher and Charlie Kelly did not sell any of the first ten Breezers. Joe sold them directly to customers at $750 for a complete bike, including a pump and a tool kit.

Left: Fig. 8.12. Three early Breezer's lined up. The one in the back is Joe's personal Mark I, while the two in front are Mark IIs, owned by Wende Cragg and Charlie Kelly respectively. Mark IIs can be recognized by their BMX-style front forks.

Left: Fig. 10.13. Joe Breeze looking at a collection of nickel-plated Mark II Breezers. The five on the left are second-generation models, without the twin-lateral tubes. Also note the variety of handlebars.

Chapter 9.
Crested Butte to Aspen
and Beyond

Reports reached Marin of a Colorado bicycle race from Crested Butte to Aspen on a rocky trail over 12,700 ft. high Pearl Pass, rumored to be held annually in September. That seemed like grist for the mill of the Marin clunker riders.

In September 1978, Joe Breeze, Mike Castelli, Wende Cragg, and Charlie Kelly drove to Crested Butte. Gary Fisher flew in from Emmaus, Pennsylvania, where he had been road testing bicycles for

Left: Fig. 9.1. View of Crested Butte, just south of Crested Butte Mountain. As the crow flies, Aspen is 30 miles from Crested Butte, but to get there, you either go over rock-strewn Pearl Pass or make an 85 mile detour on the highway.

Bicycling! magazine. Joe, Charlie, and Wende took their Breezers. Gary and Mike took their old derailleur clunkers.

Most of the Crested Butte riders were seasonal forest firefighters who did most of their training at the Grubstake Bar and Grill. They rode plain vanilla one-speed Schwinns and similar cruisers.

The history of the ride goes back to 1976, when some of the yuppie crowd from the fashionable resort town of Aspen rode their motorcycles across Pearl Pass into decidedly less sophisticated Crested Butte. Not to be outdone, 15 of the Crested Butte locals returned the favor—riding their equally unsophisticated one-speed bikes, supported by pickup trucks to carry camping gear, beer, and other essentials for the two-day trip. They celebrated their arrival in Aspen by lighting up the

Right: Fig. 9.2. The Grubstake Bar and Grill is the unofficial town hall of Crested Butte. This is where the Marin riders first met the brave cyclists of Crested Butte.

Below: Fig. 9.3. The start line-up in Crested Butte for the 1978 event.

town. For the return journey everybody (and every bike) got loaded on pickup trucks for the bone-shattering trek across the pass.

Marin Invasion

It turned out that it was more of an event than a race, and this year, 1978, the locals hadn't decided to put it on yet. However, here were five people from out of town, in-

cluding a woman, who had driven 1,000 miles from Marin to participate. The machismo kicked in, and the event was quickly scheduled.

During the transit of Pearl Pass, it became clear that the Marin derailleur bicycles with good brakes were much better suited to the terrain than the single-speed bikes ridden by the locals. It was also evident that the custom-made Breezers were more durable than the old Schwinn

Above: Figs. 9.4 & 9.5. Two typical examples of Crested Butte "Town Bikes."

Left: Fig. 9.6. Line-up at Pearl Pass Summit.

clunkers—regardless whether with or without derailleur gearing.

After the event was over, Gary Fisher pulled a wheelie on his

derailleur clunker to impress the small fry in Aspen—and his handlebars broke off...

The Crested Butte to Aspen via Pearl Pass ride was repeated in 1979, with even more Marin participants and more purpose-built mountain bikes. It has since become a regular feature, and a major mountain bike festival.

Above: Fig. 9.7. The "Bike Pile" at Crested Butte would grow from year to year.

Top left: Fig. 9.8. Mixing with the locals upon arrival in Aspen.

Bottom left: Fig. 9.9. Even in 1979, most Crested Butte locals were still riding single-speeds.

Chapter 10.
Beyond Cottage Industry

In November 1978, Gary Fisher ordered three custom clunker frames from Marin frame builder Jeff Richman. It took Jeff four months to complete the order. Gary says that he didn't order a Breezer because he didn't like the twin-lateral frame design.

About the same time, Schwinn introduced the Klunker V, which sold for $160. It had fat tires and five-speed derailleur gearing, but it was closer to a beach cruiser than a mountain bike.

Also in 1978, Mert Lawill dropped by the Koski's Cove Bike Shop in Tiburon. Mert was a motorcycle racer and builder. He talked about building a custom BMX bike. Don Koski suggested that Mert build a klunker instead. Don made a prototype from thin-walled electrical conduit to show what it should look like. This led to the design and

Left: Fig. 10.1. The Lawill-Knight ProCruiser, introduced in 1978 by Mert Lawill and inspired by Don Koski's basic design concept. Early models, like this one, had drum brakes instead of the cantilever brakes used by other builders.

production of the Lawill-Knight ProCruiser.

The First Ritchey Mountain Bikes

The demand remained for custom-built fat-tired off-road bikes. After the Breezers, it was hard to call a custom-built bike a "clunker." They were now mountain bikes by my definition—except that the term had not been coined yet.

Marin—indeed most of Northern California—had been "mined" clean of suitable old frames. Foraging expeditions to the hinterlands were coming back empty handed. Gary needed a rapid frame builder, and that frame builder would be Tom Ritchey.

In January 1979, Tom was building a tandem for Joe Breeze and Otis Guy. They planned to attempt to beat the Trans-America tandem record. Joe took a Breezer to show Tom how he wanted the twin-lateral tubes to be installed on the tandem.

Tom was already riding off-road on a lightweight bicycle with tubular tires, essentially a cyclo-cross bike. He had a project to build a lightweight off-road bicycle using 650B tires (approximately equivalent to 26 x 1.625 inch) and alloy rims. When he saw the Breezer, he put that project on hold and decided to

build his own custom clunker using the wider 26 x 2.125 tires. Tom felt that he could make a lighter bike than the Breezer by using a larger diameter downtube (1.25 mm rather than 1.125 mm diameter) instead of the twin-laterals. Tom's frame geometry was also based on that of the proven Schwinn Excelsior.

Tom rode in the January 20, 1979 Repack race on Wende Cragg's Schwinn clunker. He crashed when the handlebars twisted. This led him

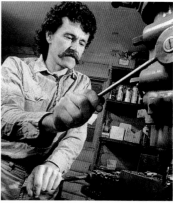

Right and below: Figs. 10.2 & 10.3. Even today, Tom Ritchey can be found machining bike parts or brazing a frame.

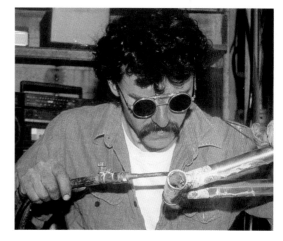

to develop what later became his signature "Bullmoose" handlebar design, which combines stem and handlebars in one welded unit.

At the race, Gary Fisher and Tom Ritchey discussed mountain bikes. There are two versions of what happened next. Gary recalls that he ordered three frames from Tom. Tom made the three frames in two weeks. Tom decided to keep one frame for himself. Gary picked up the two frames in February 1979.

Tom recalls that Gary ordered one frame. Tom made the second frame for himself, since he and Gary rode the same size, and decided to make an extra frame. This was the basis of the "one for Tom, one for Gary, and one to sell" story.

Tom was a rapid and prolific frame builder. Only 20 years old at the time, he had already established a reputation for himself as an expert frame builder, turning out about 250 road bike frames a year. He was also a skilled machinist and had a machine shop to make the exotic parts needed for custom clunkers.

There are also two versions of the story of the next batch of Ritchey frames. Tom recalls that after he completed the first three, he decided to build a second batch of nine more frames. When they were finished, he called Gary to see if he wanted to sell them.

Gary, on the other hand, recalls that he ordered ten more frames when he picked up the first two.

The nine (or ten) frames were completed in three weeks, and they were picked up in mid-March. Tom charged $450 each for painted frames with forks. Forks were time-consuming to build, and added significantly to the cost. Gary sold the 10 frames over the next three or four months, and paid Tom for the

Left: Fig. 10.4. One of the early (probably even the first) mountain bikes with Ritchey frame built for Fisher and Kelly's fledgling Mountain Bikes company.

frames as he sold the completed bicycles.

The Origins of the MountainBikes Company.

1979 was a hectic year for Gary Fisher. He was road testing bicycles for *Bicycling!* magazine. He was a serious Category One bicycle racer, and went to France for several weeks to race and train. He spent three months at the training center for the U.S. Olympic bicycle team in Colorado Springs. Eddie Borysewicz, the team coach, told Gary that he was too old and would never be a top road racer. It was time for a career change.

In the summer of 1979, Gary Fisher was returning from Palo Alto with a truckload of Ritchey frames. On the way home, he met Charlie Kelly in Fairfax. They no longer shared a house but were still friends. Gary stopped to show Charlie the new frames.

Gary needed help to handle the growing business. Then and there, they pooled their total capital (about $300), opened a joint bank account, and founded their business as a partnership. Either Charlie Kelly or Gary Fisher coined the name "MountainBikes" in September

What's the best way to travel in remote areas? The Mountain Bike goes anywhere. Silently.

Balloon tires. 18 speeds. 28 lb.

Write or call:

Mountain Bikes
Box 405
Fairfax, CA, 94930
(415) 456-1898

MOUNTAIN BIKES
P.O. Box 405
Fairfax, CA 94930
(415) 456-1898

GARY FISHER

KELLY

Above: Fig. 10.5. Now they were in business: Gary Fisher and Charlie Kelly each had their own "Mountain Bikes" business cards.

Left: Fig. 10.6. The first Mountain Bikes catalog of 1979. Note that "Mountain Bikes was written as two words, as it would remain until 1981.

1979, when they applied for a business license.

MountainBikes assembled Tom Ritchey's frames into bicycles and sold them for around $1,300, payable in advance. After you paid your money, Gary shopped around for components to complete the Ritchey-MountainBike, which is what they were called when Tom Ritchey supplied the frames.

They also bought frames from other frame builders, but Tom was their major supplier. The first MountainBikes catalogues emphasized the Ritchey name. Most people assumed that Tom Ritchey owned MountainBikes, or at least that he was a partner. This wasn't the case. Gary Fisher and Charlie Kelly owned MountainBikes. There was no written contract between MountainBikes and Tom Ritchey. Everything was done by verbal agreement. This would cause serious problems four years down the road.

Tom Ritchey was a friend of John Finley Scott. John saw the potential of the mountain bike market. He recognized the trend and planned to be a major part of it. John ordered 100 mountain bike frames from Tom Ritchey. The price was $190 for an unpainted frame without forks. When John asked for a volume discount, Tom agreed to supply 110 frames for the same price. John's huge frame order allowed Tom to build the jigs to speed up his frame building operation.

John's mountain bike sales plans did not develop as rapidly as he had hoped. It required considerable organization to make the forks, paint the frames, and assemble the bicycles. John stored most of the frames in his garage in Davis.

John knew of the MountainBikes operation in Fairfax. He approached Gary Fisher and offered to sell Gary the Ritchey frames on a pay-as-you-sell basis. John also loaned Gary $10,000 to keep the MountainBikes operation afloat.

1979 was the critical year in the growth of the mountain bike and of MountainBikes. Sales went to a few hundred. John Finley Scott's order of 110 Ritchey frames and his loan to Gary Fisher came at a critical time and kept the market growing.

The first MountainBikes used an eclectic mix of components: Huret Duopar rear derailleur, Sim-

Left: Fig. 10.7. The SunTour Mighty Shifter was the favored gear shifter on most mountain bikes sold in the 70s and early 80s.

plex front derailleur, SunTour thumb- shifters, TA Cyclotouriste triple crankset, SunTour Winner freewheel, Phil Wood hubs, Mafac tandem cantilever brakes, Magura moto-cross brake levers, and an Avocet saddle. MountainBikes was able to accumulate a small inventory of the special components, which allowed others to build their own mountain bikes.

The first mountain bikes used steel rims. In 1979, Araya and Ukai introduced 26-inch alloy rims for the adult BMX market. The aluminum rims made cantilever brakes more effective. When the CyclePro Snakebelly skin-wall mountain bike tire appeared in 1980. The new tire-rim combination took 6 pounds off the weight of the wheels. This was a huge improvement in mountain bikes. The lightest version of the 1980 Ritchey-MountainBike weighed only 28 pounds.

Awakening

In 1979, something like 200 custom-built mountain bikes were sold. This included about 40 Ritchey-MountainBikes and about 75 Mert Lawill ProCruisers. The $500 TIG-welded ProCruiser had marginal frame geometry. Other custom builders made smaller quantities.

In 1979, Schwinn changed the name of the Klunker V to Spitfire V and raised the price to $173. Estimating mountain bike sales is difficult because of bikes like the Schwinns. Were they mountain bikes, cruisers, or adult BMX bikes? Four companies exhibited mountain bikes at the Long Beach Bike Show in January 1980.

Right: Fig. 10.8. John Finley Scott helped establish the mountain bike business in general, and MountainBikes in particular. His double-decker bus carried many mountain bikes and riders to the trailhead and served as a base camp during the late 70s and early 80s.

Tom Ritchey made the first "Bullmoose" combined handlebar-stem in early 1980. Fat-tire bikes required a longer bottom bracket spindle so that the chainrings cleared the chainstay. Tom made a custom sealed-bearing bottom bracket that provided wide-spaced bearings.

In March 1980, Gary Fisher won the Reseda-to-the-Sea Challenge race on a mountain bike, and he was second in the Sacramento District Cyclo-Cross Championship on a mountain bike. These results illuminated that the mountain bike was more than just a downhill racer.

About 150 Ritchey-Mountain-Bikes were sold in 1980. This was probably half the total sales of genuine mountain bikes. Joe Breeze made and sold 25 Breezers in 1980 and 1981. The second-generation Breezers had an oversize downtube instead of twin-lateral tubes.

The Spread of Mountain Biking

Fifteen custom builders exhibited mountain bikes at the January 1981 Long Beach Bicycle Trade Show. The same year, the first mountain bike races in Southern California were held.

Tom Ritchey had two part-time employees who prepared the tubing, but he did all the frame brazing himself. Tom made six different mountain bike frame sizes. He would

Above: Fig. 10.9. Tom Ritchey's signature "Bullmoose" handlebars combined stem and bars in one welded unit.

Right: Fig. 10.10. The closest thing to a mountain bike that Schwinn could come up with at the time was the Sidewinder, which was based on a Schwinn Varsity frame, just like John Finely Scott's 1953 Woodsy bike.

make a batch of 100 frames in one size and then take a few weeks off before making a batch of a different size.

John Finley Scott purchased Spence Wolfe's Cupertino Bike Shop in January 1981. It became the headquarters for mountain bike sales south of San Francisco. Gary Fisher repaid his loan from John with finished Ritchey-Mountain-Bikes, which were sold at the Cupertino Bike Shop.

The Specialized Stumpjumper

Mike Sinyard's company, Specialized Bicycle Imports (SBI), sold imported parts to MountainBikes. Mike could see the growing market. He recalls that in mid-1981 he bought a Ritchey-MountainBike for his personal use, and three more for his friends.

Mike and his designer, Tim Neenan, liked those bikes so much, that Mike decided to import a Japa-nese-made mountain bike. Tim suggested minor design changes. Mike took his Ritchey-MountainBike and Neenan's drawings to Japan and ordered copies from Toyo, the company that was building road bikes for SBI.

There is an interesting story about these bikes. Many Ritchey frames did not include forks, so the forks were made by other frame builders. Forks were time-consuming because no fork crowns were available in the right size. Tom's frames had a sloping top tube. John Paget was one of the frame builders who made forks. He assumed that the frames had a level top tube and he made a batch of forks that were about half an inch too long. Gary and Charlie needed to make deliveries, so they used the forks anyway. This resulted in extra fender clear-

Right: Fig. 10.11. The 1982 Specialized Stumpjumper was the first mass-produced mountain bike to be sold nationwide. It was equipped with SunTour AR derailleurs, SunTour thumb-shifters, Mafac cantilever brakes, and a TA Cyclotouriste triple crankset.

ance and a slightly shallower head angle. The bike that Mike bought had the long forks, and this shows in the first Stumpjumpers.

The mountain bike gospel spread far beyond Marin. There were numerous organized races in the western states. The Fisher-Kelly-Ritchey operation sold about 500 Ritchey-MountainBikes in 1981. They had lots of competition from other small builders, but Mountain-Bikes was the clear leader. The Ritchey frameset sold retail for $625. A complete bike was $1,300.

In 1981 Schwinn introduced its King Sting 5. It looked like a five-speed adult BMX bike and sold for $550. Also in 1981 Murray brought out its Baja model, It sold like hot cakes at $120. With fat tires and ten-speed derailleur gearing, it looked like a mountain bike but the frame and components were gas-pipe quality.

About twenty small makers exhibited at the January 1982 Long Beach bicycle show or advertised in the 1982 *Fat Tire Flyer*. These included:

❑ Joe Breeze (Breezer)

❑ Colorado Bicycle Co. (Roughrider)

❑ Charlie Cunningham (Indian)

❑ Richard Cunningham (Mantis)

❑ Cupertino Bike Shop (Saturn)

❑ Barry Konig (Proteus)

❑ Erik Koski (Trailmaster)

❑ Mert Lawill (ProCruiser)

❑ Jeff Lindsay (Mountain Goat)

❑ Moots Cycle (Mountaineer)

❑ Scott Nicol (Ibis)

❑ Glenn Odell (Bruiser)

❑ Chris Pauley (Tierra)

❑ Steve Potts (Wilderness Trail Bikes)

❑ Mike Rust (Rocky Mountain Bicycle Works)

❑ Angel Rodriguez (R&E Cycles)

Left: Fig. 10.12. As early as 1979 Charles Cunningham was building bikes like this, with a lightweight welded and stress-relieved aluminum frame and very elegant straight-blade forks—at a price...

- Erik Sampson (Rock Creek Cycles)

- Ross Shaffer (Salsa)

- Victor Vicente of America (VVA).

- Cook Brothers

Most of those small custom builders sold direct to the customer. You paid $300 down and got your bike a few weeks or months later.

The Koskis started making Trailmaster mountain bikes with TIG-welded chrome-moly frames in late 1980. A total of 70 Trailmasters were made and sold from the Cove Bicycle Shop over the next few years.

The Fisher-Kelly-Ritchey MountainBikes operation was unique. Almost all of the frames were hand-built by Tom Ritchey, but his quantities approached factory production levels. Five hundred Ritchey-MountainBikes were sold in 1982. Prices ranged from $820 for a Ritchey Mount Tam to $1,500 for a Ritchey Everest.

Right: Fig. 10.13. Soon fter itroducing their popular straight-bladed for, the Cook Brothers started building their own brand of mountain bikes

Wilderness Trail Bikes

In 1982, Charlie Cunningham, Steve Potts, and Mark Slate combined talents and resources to form Wilderness Trail Bikes (WTB). Over the next 25 years, WTB would become a major force in mountain bike innovation. They sold Charlie Cunningham's aluminum-framed mountain bikes and Steve Pott's steel-framed mountain bikes.

They also developed Speedmaster Roller Cam brakes and Grease Guard hubs, bottom brackets, and headsets. They became a major factor in mountain bike tire design. Today, Charlie Cunningham and Steve Potts have left WTB, and the company no longer sells bicycles. Patrick Seidler, their lawyer, now runs WTB, and the main products are tires, saddles, and rims.

Chapter 11.
Mountain Bikes Enter the
Mass Market

Nineteen-eighty-two was the last year that the small custom builders dominated the market. There was a significant change at the January 1982 Long Beach Bicycle Show. Three major bike makers—Specialized, Univega, and Schwinn—displayed factory-made mountain bikes that were available at regular bike shops across America.

Mike Sinyard's $750 Specialized Stumpjumper was the talk of the show. He imported only 500 (or 1,200, there are conflicting accounts of the actual figure) in 1982. Mike could have sold many more, but there were shortages of financing and of components.

The Stumpjumper used a TA triple crankset and Mafac cantilever brakes, but the frames and other components were all made in Japan.

Left: Fig. 11.1. The $500 Univega Alpina Sport, introduced in 1982, was the best-selling mountain bike. It was equipped with SunTour Cyclone GT derailleurs and Mighty shifters, a Sugino Pro-Max double crankset, and Dia-Compe cantilever brakes.

Specialized was an effective marketer. They advertised widely and expanded the mass market for mountain bikes.

Ben Lawee of Univega imported and sold as many as 2,000 (or 3,000 —again, there are conflicting accounts of the actual numbers) of its Univega Alpina Sport mountain bikes. They were made in Japan by Araya, who also provided the frame design. The 1982 Alpina Sport had a 48–36 double chainring, so it wasn't much of a hill climber, but it only cost $500. Ben Lawee, who owned Univega, was famous for picking hot trends. The next year, Univega imported four Japanese mountain bike models made by Miyata.

Schwinn had two 1982 fat-tire offerings—the King Sting and the Sidewinder. Schwinn couldn't decide if they were mountain bikes, adult BMX bikes, or heavy-duty cruisers. Both were available with one-, five-, or ten-speed gearing, but they had inadequate brakes,

Above: Fig. 11.2. The 1983 Specialized Stumpjumper Sport had a Taiwan-made frame. Note the Bullmoose handlebars.

Bottom left: Fig. 11.3. The 1982 Schwinn King-Sting 5 was a 5-speed with a SunTour AG rear derailleur and the largest sprocket had 38 teeth. It wasn't much of a mountain bike.

Below: Fig. 11.4. This Taiwan-made MountainBikes Montare was the middle model, which sold for $610. It used SunTour MounTech derailleurs.

high-rise handlebars, and poor frame geometry. Schwinn was having serious problems, and they missed the swing to mountain bikes.

By 1983, the mountain bike was in the mainstream. Mountain bikes made up about five percent of 1983 U.S. bicycle sales. In 1983, there were "bicycles" (which at the time meant road bikes) and "mountain bikes." Ten years later, the proportions were reversed. Mountain bikes and hybrids had 95 percent of the adult market and road bikes had less than five percent. In 1993, there were "bicycles" (which meant mountain bikes) and "road bikes."

In 1983, you could still buy mountain bikes from the small custom builders, but almost all of the major

Above: Fig.11.5. Shimano representatives getting inspiration for mountain bike components at the Cove Bike Shop in 1982. From left to right, standing: Ken Fujimura, Andy O'Connor, and "Sam" Kawabata from Shimano, Mrs. Koski, Don Koski, Mr. Koski, Mr. Yamane, and Mr. Hontani; kneeling: Shimano sales rep John Uhte, Erik Koski, and Dave Koski.

Top left: Fig. 11.6. Tom Ritchey explaining his quick-release seat clamp to Junzo Kawai, President of SunTour at the 1982 Long Beach bicycle trade show.

Bottom left: Fig. 11.7. Junzo Kawai learning about mountain biking requirements from Joe Breeze at Crested Butte in 1982.

makers were in the market. Centu-rion, CyclePro, Diamondback, Fuji, KHS, Miyata, Puch, Raleigh of Amer-ica, Ross, Schwinn, Sekai, SR, Takara, Trek, and Univega all supplied moun-tain bikes at various price levels to their dealer networks. AMF, Huffy, and Murray Ohio were supplying in-expensive gas-pipe-quality ersatz mountain bikes to big-box stores.

Top right: Fig. 11.8. The 1983 Shimano Deore XT gruppo. Deore XT came out about six months late, so SunTour got most of the 1983 market. However, Deore XT held up much better to severe mountain biking, and soon captured most of the business.

Center right: Fig. 11.9. The 1983 SunTour Dirt Gruppo. The MounTech rear derailleur shifted splendidly, but it wore out after a few months of serious riding in the dirt.

Below left and right: Figs. 11.10 & 11.11. The Sugino crankset and the Dia-Compe brake set were included in the 1983 SunTour Dirt gruppo.

The Japanese component companies, especially SunTour, had closely followed the mountain bike trend. In 1983, SunTour introduced MounTech, and Shimano introduced Deore XT mountain bike gruppos. Sugino and Sakae-Ringyo (SR) introduced triple-chainring cranksets for mountain bikes. The window of opportunity for Huret, Mafac, Simplex, and TA had been wide open for five years. Now it slammed shut, and although at least TA is still around, they all missed the mountain bike boat.

Specialized introduced the $500 Stumpjumper Sport to go with the $750 Stumpjumper. The frame was made in Taiwan by Giant, but all other components were made in Japan. It sported a bullnoose handlebar, similar to Tom Ritchey's.

Gary Fisher and Tom Ritchey went to Japan together and contracted to have a less expensive MountainBike model called Montare. It was made by Matsushita Electrical Industrial Co. (Panasonic) The Montare was available in three models, priced from $450 to $750.

The Unraveling of the Fisher-Kelly-Ritchey Arrangement

In early 1983, Gary Fisher and Charlie Kelly changed the name of their company to Kelly-Fisher MountainBikes. There never was a formal written agreement with Tom Ritchey. Other custom builders had also supplied frames to Mountain-Bikes. If the frame was made by Tom Ritchey, the bicycle was called a Ritchey-MountainBike. Ritchey's name on the decal certainly added value to a MountainBike.

Tom Ritchey's company was called Ritchey Custom Cycles, but by 1983 Tom was largely out of the custom frame building business. He

Fig. 11.12. A group of SunTour managers admire Charles Cunningham's aluminum-frame mountain bike, while Charles looks on. This bike had prototype roller-cam brakes and drop handlebars.

made two grades of mountain bike frames. The top quality frames became the $1,800 Ritchey Everest or the $1,100 Ritchey McKinley. The less expensive frames became the $875 Ritchey Mount Tam. Even with the Japanese competition, about 1,000 Ritchey-MountainBikes were sold in 1983.

MountainBikes had a serious financial problem. As they grew, they hired more employees, bought more components, carried more inventory, and went deeper into debt. They were later and later in their frame payments to Tom, who was their major creditor.

In mid-1983, Gary Fisher bought out Charlie Kelly for $2,300 and an Apple computer. The price was low because MountainBikes was so deeply in debt.

Both Gary Fisher and Tom Ritchey had plans for the future, but their plans were quite different. At the end of 1983, their disagreements came to a head, and the breakup was less than amicable.

Above: Fig. 11.13. As late as February 1983, Fisher and Kelly operated under the name "Mountain Bikes" and prominently featured Tom Ritchey's name.

Left: Fig. 11.14. Later the same year they changed the company's name "Kelly-Fisher MountainBikes"

AVAILABLE NOW!

Kelly-Fisher MountainBikes

THE HOT NEW CATALOG FROM

K & F MOUNTAINBIKES

—— MOUNTAINBIKES · PARTS · ACCESSORIES ——

Send $1 to: K & F MountainBikes
1501 San Anselmo Ave., San Anselmo, CA 94960

Chapter 12.
Mountain Bike Predecessors

The publication of the first edition of *The Birth of Dirt* spurred numerous magazine articles and letters disputing my basic conclusion that no one invented the mountain bike.

In this chapter, we'll look at some of the earlier bicycles that were similar to the mountain bike, and suitable for off-road riding, but don't meet my criteria for the mountain bike.

Virtually all of the bicycles that were made in the three decades after the introduction of the pneumatic tire (I. e. between 1890 and 1920) were "bad roads bikes." They all had balloon tires, because the roads were so bad, especially in America.

Jacques Jiel-Laval's 1891 Paris–Brest–Paris Racer

The first Paris-Brest-Paris race was a test of both men and tires. The winner, Charles Terront, covered the 750 miles in 71 hours. He was sponsored by Michelin. Jacques Jiel-Laval, who came in 7 hours later in second place, was sponsored by

Left: Fig.12.1. Jacques Jiel-Laval and his ten pace riders showing off his fat-tire bike after the 1891 Paris-Brest-Paris race. No derailleur gearing and questionable brakes.

Dunlop. The race was a major triumph for pneumatic tires. At that time, the Dunlop tire was about 2 inches in diameter, so it certainly qualified as a fat tire.

Vélocio's 1905 Chainless Touricyclette

Vélocio was the pen name of Paul de Vivie. He published the magazine *Le Cycliste* from 1888 to 1923, and was known as the "Father of Multiple Gearing." His Touricyclette had fat tires, two speeds, flat handlebars and decent brakes, but it certainly wasn't a mountain bike.

Vernon Blake's 1930 Roadster

Vernon Blake was a fascinating character and a friend and protege of Vélocio. As an editor for the British

magazine *Cycling*, he had a major influence on U.K. bicycle developments.

Blake and Vélocio both believed in the *chaine flotante*, or floating chain. "Flotantistes" used two or three chainrings and a single-sprocket freewheel. The lower run of chain hung loose. Downshifts were made by kicking the chain with the heel. Upshifts by lifting the chain with a wire hook or a finger.

Above: Fig. 12.2. Vélocio with his 1905 Touricyclette. Fat tires, flat handlebars, 2-speed gearing (and shaft drive)—yet it's not a mountain bike.

Left: Fig. 12.3. Vernon Blake's 1930 Bad Roads bicycle. Fat tires, flat handlebars, "floating chain" gearing, decent brakes, but a mountain bike it wasn't.

In the May 1930 CTC Gazette, Blake described a bicycle that he made for bad roads and long hills. It used 26 x 2 inch balloon tires. The gear-train used 48-36-24 chainrings and a reversible rear wheel with a 16-tooth sprocket on one side and an 18-tooth on the other. It had roadster handlebars, cantilever brakes, and handmade brake levers.

Was this the first mountain bike? Would it have been the first mountain bike if Vernon Blake had fitted derailleurs? Probably not. The problem was not lack of technical features, but timing. Blake was premature and nothing came of his

bicycle. In 1930, the cycling world wasn't ready for mountain bikes.

French Touring Bicycles of the 1920s and 1930s

Led by Vélocio and the Federation Française des Societies de Cyclo-tourisme (FFSC), the French developed practical touring bikes suitable

Right: Fig. 12.4. The 1920s Hirondelle Retro-Directe had flat handlebars, wide tires, and powerful centerpull brakes. The geartrain used a front derailleur, which gave two gears pedaling forward and two lower gears pedaling backward.

Left: Fig. 12.5. This RPF "Grand Touring" bicycle from France was first available in 1928. It had Cyclo front and rear derailleurs, wide-range gearing, cantilever brakes and balloon tires.

for rough roads. These bikes had wide-range derailleur gearing, powerful brakes, and relatively fat tires ($1^3/_4$ to 2 in. wide). The French did not believe in skinny tires for touring. Most had drop handlebars for more choices in hand position, but some had flat handlebars. Because the Marin developers had never seen them, these bikes were not progenitors of the mountain bike.

French Vélo-Cross Racing in the 1950s

In the mid 1950s, a number of young Frenchmen decided to race bicycles on the moto-cross courses near Paris. They formed the Vélo-Cross Club de Paris to support their sport. They built special bicycles with derailleur gearing, disc brakes, flat handlebars and front suspension.

These bicycles had all of the technical features of the 1970s mountain bikes. Their front suspension and disk brakes were decades ahead of the Marin mountain bikes. However, the Vélo-Cross sport failed to attract public interest, and

Fig. 12.6. The Vélo-Cross Club de Paris was active in France between 1951 and 1956. This is the kind of bike the members rode.

Left: Fig. 12.7. In 1953 John Finley Scott converted a Schwinn Varsity into this "Woodsy Bike."

it died out, along with those sophisticated pre-mountain bikes.

John Finley Scott's Woodsy Bikes of 1953 and 1960

John Finley Scott was a bicycle innovator. As an undergraduate student in 1953 he assembled a 9-speed fat-tire, "Woodsy" bike using a Schwinn Varsity frame, flat handlebars and a hybrid gear-train with a Sturmey-Archer 3-speed hub, an 18 to 28 three-sprocket freewheel, and a Super Champion rear derailleur. He proved to himself that with low enough gearing, it was possible to ride over rough single-track trails. This bike was stolen, but in subsequent years he built more bikes like it.

The 1960 version of his Woodsy Bike had a custom-built Jeff Butter frame with 650B rims and tires, drop handlebars, sidepull brakes, Cyclo Benelux rear derailleur, Simplex front derailleur, a TA 52-49-30 triple crankset, and a 14 to 28 five-sprocket freewheel.

John pedaled this bike thousands of miles over numerous high mountain passes. John shows up again in the mountain bike story in 1979 when he bought 110 frames from Tom Ritchey and provided the initial financing for Gary Fisher's operation.

John's Woodsy Bikes met almost all of the technical requirements of a mountain bike but the cycling world wasn't ready for mountain bikes yet.

Schwinn Corvette of 1961–1962

Frank W. Schwinn believed in derailleur bicycles: The problem was educating the American market. The 1961–1962 Corvette was a five-speed derailleur version of a popular middleweight Schwinn bicycle. It had middleweight tires, flat handle bars,

Left: Fig 12.8. The 1961 Schwinn Corvette had 26 x 1.75 in. tires, and was offered with five-speed derailleur gearing, as shown here. This bike had the Schwinn "cantilever" frame design, which did not hold up as well as the old Excelsior frame design.

derailleur gears, and moderately effective caliper brakes. It sold poorly when ten-speed Schwinn Varsities and Continentals were selling well. With chrome fenders and front and rear racks, the Corvette was clearly not designed for off-road use.

Tim DuPertuis' 1972 24-Inch Clunker

In the spring of 1972, Tim DuPertuis was working in the Boneshaker bike shop in San Anselmo. He built a fat-tire bike for his own use with front and rear derailleurs.

Tim was only 5 feet 5 inches tall, so he used a youth frame with 24-inch wheels. This may have been the first fat-tire bike in Marin with derailleur gearing. It had poor brakes, and "ape- hanger" handlebars.

Tim had this bike for only two months before he sold it. No one from the Velo-Club Tamalpais recalls seeing it. It was just another of the numerous fat-tired derailleur bikes that came to nothing. When he got back from a long trip to Europe, Tim built another fat-tired bike, this time with a Sturmey Archer 3-speed hub and drum brakes.

Right: Fig. 12.9. This is Tim DuPertuis' second geared clunker. Whereas No. 1 had derailleur gearing, this one has Sturmey-Archer hub gearing instead of derailleurs. This photo was taken at Joe Breeze's 20-year anniversary party in 1997.

Chapter 13.
The "Mountain Bike" Name

There is still some dispute over the origin of the name Mountain Bike. So in this chapter we'll trace the history of use of this term, and specifically in connection with the bike we now know as the mountain bike.

Probably the first mention of something on the lines of "mountain bike" was the caption for a drawing that appeared in the a German magazine *Fliegende Blaetter* in 1869.

The drawing was captioned "Gebirgevelocipede" (German for "mountain bike") and showed a balloon-supported bicycle. An interesting artist's conception, but it could not possibly have been put into practice. Nevertheless, it was probably the first use of the term "mountain bike."

In the mid 1970s, a Santa Barbara hippie called Wing Bamboo used the term "mountain bike" to

Left and facing page: Figs. 13.1 and 13.2. Two German cartoons from a 1896 issue of *Fliegende Blaetter*, showing concepts for a "Gelaendevelociped," or off-road bicycle.

describe his own fat-tire clunker. James McLean, who at the time was a salesman for Specialized, heard Wing Bamboo use the name, and he suggested it to Charlie Kelly in 1978.

Either Charlie Kelly or Gary Fisher coined the name "Mountain-Bike" (written as one word, but with a capital B in the middle) in September 1979, when they took out a Marin County fictitious name business license in the name "Mountain-Bikes." In the early catalogs it was spelled variously "Mountain Bikes" (two words) and MountainBikes" (one word).

In 1980, Charlie Kelly hired a lawyer to trademark the name. They applied for trademarks for "Moun-tainBike," "Mountainbike," "Moun-tain Bike," and "mountain bike." The trademark office asked if the bike was only for mountain use. The lawyer said "yes," but the correct answer would have been "no," so the trademark application was re-jected. Gary and Charlie did not mention their failure to get a trade-mark at the time. It was generally as-sumed that they had a trademark.

Gary's and Charlie's Mountain-Bikes operation was the first to use the name to describe their fat-tire bi-cycles, and they are the ones who popularized the name "mountain bike."

The final insult came when *Bicy-cling!* magazine decided that "moun-tain bike" was unsuitable as a generic name, and held a contest for

Above: Fig. 13.3. In their 1979 ads and sales brochures, the name "Mountain Bikes" was spelled in two words.

a better name. The winner was "ATB," or All Terrain Bike. The editors of *Bicycling!* decreed that henceforth mountain bikes would be called ATBs. This caused confusion for three or four years, but the public wouldn't buy the ATB name. Today, mountain bike is the generic name for a derailleur-geared fat-tire bike.

It is interesting to note that Gary Fisher had another somewhat curious brush with the use of a name. When he chose the name Fisher Mountain Bikes for his business, that name was challenged by the Austrian ski manufacturer Fischer. Although "Fisher" was not the same as "Fischer," and although the

Fischer company never made bicycles of any kind (neither before the incident, nor since), the judge ruled against Gary's use of his own last name. Finally, he settled on the name Gary Fisher Mountain Bikes (and later Gary Fisher Bicycles). From a PR standpoint, that turned out to be a happy ending for Gary Fisher.

Left and above: Figs. 13.4 & 13.5. Pre- and post-Fisher-Kelly-Ritchey unraveling. Ritchey's name was featured prominently on MountainBikes' advertising right up to early 1983. Later that same year it was abruptly changed to "Kelly-Fisher MountainBikes."

Chapter 14.
Looking at the Numbers

In this chapter we'll take a look at the development of the early mountain bike industry by counting the number of bicycles that were made year by year from the beginnings of the sport in 1973 until the start of mass production in 1983.

Table 14.1. Development of mountain bike inventory, 1943–1983

Year	Derailleur Clunkers	Mountain Bikes	Remarks
1973	3	0	Cupertino clunkers
1974	3	0	Cupertino clunkers
1975	5	0	Marin clunkers
1976	20–100	0	Marin clunkers
1977	100+	2	Almost all in Marin
1978	100+	9	Almost all in Marin
1979	N/A	200	Mostly in Marin
1980	N/A	300	Mostly in SF Bay area
1981	N/A	2,000	Nationwide
1982	N/A	5,000	Nationwide
1983	N/A	50,000	Nationwide

Table 14.1 summarizes my attempt to estimate the production figures for derailleur clunkers and purpose-built mountain bikes over the 11-year period from 1973 through 1983.

This table roughly shows the growth of clunkers and mountain bikes in the San Francisco Bay Area for the first eight years. From 1981 onward, we are looking at nationwide sales of mountain bikes.

From 1973 to 1978, the table shows the approximate numbers of fat-tired derailleur-geared bikes with old frames (derailleur clunkers). From 1979 to 1983, the table counts new custom-built frames (mountain bikes) that were made both in the Bay Area and elsewhere. The figures are approximations, because nobody kept a good count and because of the problem of separating the *ersatz* mountain-bikes like the Murray Baja from the genuine articles.

Above: Fig. 14.2. Looks like a mountain bike, even says so on the downtube. However, though not as bad as a Murray Baja, this was still junk.

Left: Fig. 14.3. A group of early mountain bikers on a "mountain high."

Chapter 15.
Summary of the Chronology

Here is a brief summary of the significant events that led to the mountain bike. The total time span is divided up into a number of periods, each characterized by a distinct development stage.

1970–1976: The Clunker Stage

❑ 1970: Larkspur Canyon Gang members ride balloon-tired coaster-brake clunkers on Mount Tamalpais in Marin.

❑ 1972: Russ Mahon and others in the Morrow Dirt Club ride balloon-tired clunkers with derailleur gearing in the Cupertino area.

❑ 1972: Tim DuPertuis builds a 24-inch-wheel clunker with derailleurs in Marin.

❑ 1975: Gary Fisher, Marc Vendetti, Otis Guy, Alan Bonds, and others build derailleur clunkers with good brakes, 5-sprocket freewheels, front and rear derailleurs, and double-chainwheel cranksets.

1976–1980: Custom-Built Mountain Bikes

❑ 1976: Craig Mitchell makes a custom-built mountain bike frame for Charlie Kelly.

❑ 1977: Joe Breeze builds ten complete mountain bikes with new frames and new components, cantilever brakes, front and rear derailleurs, thumb-shifters, and triple cranksets.

❑ 1979: Tom Ritchey builds Ritchey frames, assembled into

mountain bikes by Gary Fisher and Charlie Kelly.

❑ 1979: Gary Fisher and Charlie Kelly make first commercial use of the name "MountainBike."

❑ 1980: Several small bike shops and frame builders make mountain bikes.

Mass-Produced Mountain Bikes

❑ 1982: Mike Sinyard (Specialized Stumpjumper) and Ben Lawee (Univega Alpina Sport) introduce mass-produced mountain bikes built in Japan for regular retail distribution.

❑ 1983 onward: Major bike companies make mass-produced mountain bikes sold in regular bike shops.

Three stages of mountain bike development:

Top left: Fig. 15.1. An early-geared clunker: The bike Gary Fisher built for Bob Burrowes.

Top right Fig. 15.2. An early custom-built mountain bike: A 1979 Koski Trailmaster.

Bottom right: Fig. 15.3. The first mass-produced real mountain bike: the 1981 Specialized Stumpjumper.

Chapter 16.
So, Who Done It?

Gary Fisher had long claimed to have invented the mountain bike. None of the other pioneers whom I interviewed claimed to be the inventor, but they all felt Gary was not the inventor either.

The Candidates

Depending on the definition of "inventor," there are three possible choices:

1. **Did John Finley Scott invent the mountain bike?**

❑ His "Woodsy Bikes" had all of the essential features.
  However, I don't consider him the inventor of the mountain bike because they were made for his personal use and nothing came of them.

2. **Did Russ Mahon invent the mountain bike?**

❑ He made the first fat-tire off-road bikes with all of the essential features in February 1973. He assembled three off-road bikes with derailleur gearing and his friends assembled more and used them in the Cupertino area. Gary Fisher saw Russ's bike in December 1974.
  I don't consider Russ Mahon the inventor of the mountain bike, because he had nothing further to do with mountain bike developments after 1974, and off-road riding died out in the Cupertino area.

3. **Or did Gary Fisher invent the mountain bike?**

- ❑ He never produced any evidence to support his claim that he fitted a freewheel and a rear derailleur to his Schwinn clunker in September 1974—before he saw Russ Mahon's "Cupertino bikes." There is considerable evidence to support a mid-1975 date for Gary's first derailleur clunker.

Analysis of Gary Fisher's Claim

Assuming that Gary made his first derailleur-equipped bike in mid-1975, after he had seen Russ Mahon's bikes, Gary can not be the inventor of the mountain bike, because he did not have the brainstorm for his first derailleur clunker until he saw the derailleur-equipped Cupertino clunkers in 1974. After that, he added derailleurs to his own

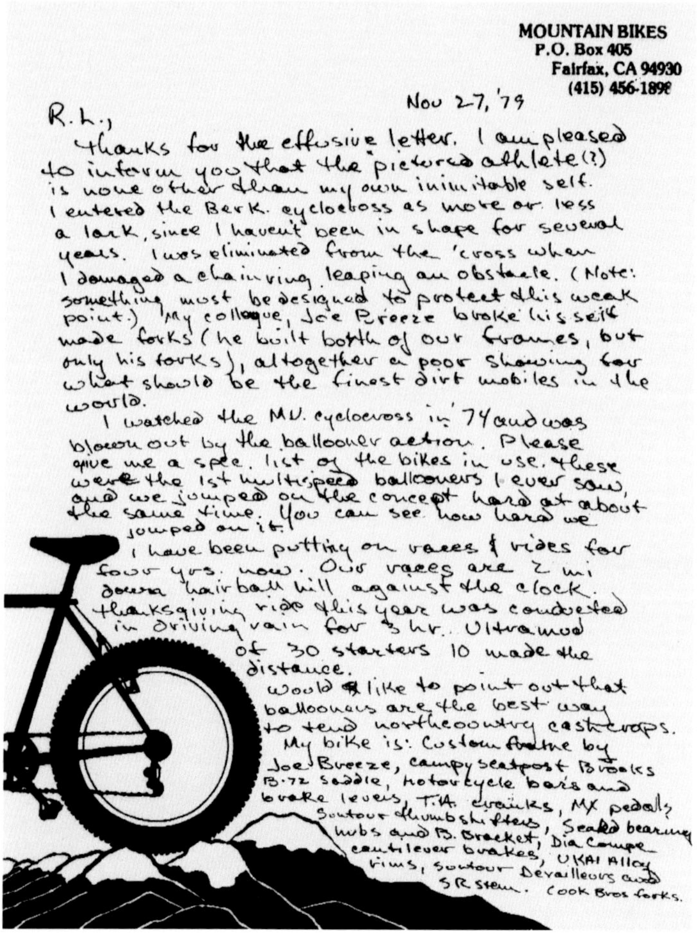

MOUNTAIN BIKES
P.O. Box 405
Fairfax, CA 94930
(415) 456-1898

Nov 27, '79

R.L.,

thanks for the effusive letter. I am pleased to inform you that the pictured athlete(?) is none other than my own inimitable self. I entered the Berk. cyclocross as more or less a lark, since I haven't been in shape for several years. I was eliminated from the 'cross when I damaged a chainring leaping an obstacle. (Note: something must be designed to protect this weak point.) My collegue, Joe Breeze broke his self made forks (he built both of our frames, but only his forks), altogether a poor showing for what should be the finest dirt mobiles in the world.

I watched the M.V. cyclocross in '74 and was blown out by the ballooner action. Please give me a spec. list of the bikes in use. these were the 1st multispeed ballooners I ever saw, and we jumped on the concept hard at about the same time. You can see how hard we jumped on it.

I have been putting on races & rides for four yrs. now. Our races are 2 mi down hairball hill against the clock. thanksgiving ride this year was conducted in driving rain for 3 hr. Ultramud of 30 starters 10 made the distance.

would like to point out that ballooners are the best way to tend northcountry cashcrops.

My bike is: Custom frame by Joe Breeze, campy seatpost Brooks B-72 saddle, motorcycle bars and brake levers, T.A. cranks, MX pedals, Suntour thumbshifters, Sealed bearing hubs and B. Bracket, Dia Compe cantilever brakes, UKAI Alloy rims, Suntour Derailleurs and SR stem. Cook Bros forks.

Fig.16.1. This is a letter Charlie Kelly wrote on Mountain Bikes letterhead in 1979. It clearly confirms that the Cupertino bikes at the 1974 cyclo-cross race were the first derailleur-geared clunkers anybody in Marin had seen. Gary's Fisher's claim of having built such a bike before that date appears to have been "invented" in later years.

clunker. However, Gary Fisher does meet the other four criteria to qualify as the inventor according to my definition:

❑ He assembled the first derailleur clunker in Marin with all of the key mountain bike features.

❑ His 1975 clunker was the progenitor of today's mountain bikes.

❑ He was actively linked to the progression of events that led to the development of the mountain bike.

❑ He (and/or his partner Charlie Kelly) first popularized what has since become the generic name "mountain bike."

So, Nobody Done It?

Right. My conclusion is that no one person invented the mountain bike. Mountain bikes just happened when enough of the early pioneers piled enough developmental logs on to the mountain bike bonfire. Critical mass was achieved and the mountain bike mushroomed. Nobody invented the mountain bike. The mountain bike just developed, and it happened in Marin County in the early 1970s.

Above and left: Figs. 16.2 & 16.3. Former business partners Gary Fisher (above) and Charlie Kelly (left) suggest different dates for the same facts concerning the origins of the mountain bike. All available evidence points to the conclusion that Kelly's is the more credible account.

Chapter 17.
Lessons for Cycling Historians

As mentioned in the introduction, there is an interesting parallel between the disputes about the invention of the mountain bike and those about the invention of the velocipede more than a century earlier.

The velocipede was the first pedal-driven bicycle. That time around,

the names were not Fisher, Mahon, or Scott but Pierre and Ernest Michaux, Lallement, and the Olivier brothers.

It had long been assumed that the father, Pierre Michaux, was the inventor of the velocipede. Without a doubt he was the first to exploit the idea, together with his son Ernest. It is notable that the Olivier brothers were at least the financial backers, if not the brains behind the operation and the application of the

Left: Fig. 17.1. A bitter publicity battle was fought in France to erect this monument to Pierre and Ernest Michaux, though they almost certainly did not invent the velocipede in 1855 as claimed.

idea. Meanwhile, Pierre Lallement made a velocipede and was the first person to patent the idea.

So how does my analysis of the origins of the mountain bike parallel this earlier historical dispute about the invention of the velocipede in the 1860s?

My first observation is that people have poor memories for dates. Even though the events that led to today's mountain bike took place less than 40 years ago and all of the principals are still alive, I found it difficult to fix dates within a year. It was necessary to read letters, catalogs, and magazines to fix correct dates.

The most reliable dating mechanism is the publication date of the literature. We can be sure that an event took place before the date of publication of literature that described the event. The later the pub-

lication, the greater the likelihood that the author is repeating old myths or inventing new ones.

The most interesting parallel is between Gary Fisher and Pierre Michaux. Pierre Michaux (or the later historians) had to predate Michaux's invention of the velocipede back to either 1855 or 1861 to predate Lallement's 1863 velocipede. Gary Fisher tried to predate his first derailleur-equipped clunker from mid-1975 back to September 1974 to precede his known sighting of Russ Mahon's derailleur-equipped clunker. Pierre Michaux needed to rewrite history by eight years or so. Gary Fisher needed less than a year.

The invention of the mountain bike has a serious problem because it was a combination of features, and there were many similar earlier bicycles. This is less of a problem with

Fig. 17.2. This machine, created in 1869 by Meyer-Guilmet in France, had all the features of a modern safety bicycle—more than a dozen years before the launch of James Starley's Rover. In fact, Meyer-Guilmet was also first in the use of tension-spoked wheels.

the velocipede. We eliminate Kirk-patrick Macmillan's presumed 1842 invention by saying it was not pedal-driven.

Few inventions take place without something similar having been invented before. Does the inventor's original brainstorm have to be virginal? If the inventor didn't know about the prior device, can he still be the inventor? Is it the existence of the prior device or the inventor's awareness of the prior device that is critical? Dictionary definitions don't help us in these areas.

Historians must decide if the previous bicycles were essentially the same as the inventor's bicycle. "Velocipede" and "mountain bike" must be precisely defined to establish if the invented bicycle was different from the earlier bicycles.

If the later velocipede or mountain bike was essentially the same as the earlier one, and if the maker of the later bicycle was aware of the earlier bicycle, then we have to assume that he copied the earlier bicycle and that he is not the inventor. The dictionary definition for "invent" requires originality.

Other Requirements for Invention

Finally, we have to decide if the inventor actively pursued his invention. The dictionary definitions give us some help here. An inventor must fabricate subsequent devices.

My litmus test is that the inventor's first device should be the progenitor of the line of later devices. There are three cumulative requirements: the original idea, the first prototype, and the subsequent development. This often leads to the situation where there is no inventor, because no one person meets all three requirements.

Fig. 17.3. Alexandre Lefèbvre's lever-driven machine has been variously dated from 1843 to 1861. It is another case of "post-factum dating," and so far there is no conclusive evidence to determine whether it qualifies as an "invention."

Chapter 18.
Response from Gary Fisher

When I had completed the final draft of my paper "Who Invented the Mountain Bike" at the 8th International Cycle History Conference in the summer of 1998, I sent copies to the main "characters." After reading it, Gary Fisher sent me a letter by fax.

Gary's letter is reproduced in full on the next page. Although it was neither signed nor dated, it seems to settle the issue once and for all: Gary Fisher accepts that he will not go down in history as the "inventor" of the mountain bike.

What is perhaps the most significant—and too easily forgotten—issue is the one revealed in the last paragraph of this letter: Gary's reminder to all of us historians who

Right: Fig. 18.1. One thing all the mountain bike pioneers could at least agree on: Having fun was the best aspect of "inventing" the mountain bike.

tend to take the whole thing too seriously.

"One aspect of the story I don't think you mentioned was how much fun the development was. The mountain bike was a secret, that once shared, changed people's lives forever. To watch it spread, bringing joy to the world made my contemporaries and I (sic) feel like true contributors to society."

Frank Berto's Comments on Gary Fisher's Letter

A book about Middle East oil explained why the French national oil company was kicked out of Iraq and the British national oil company was kicked out of Iran, but the American oil companies still have a presence in Saudi Arabia. It said that the American oil companies had "the

---

Dear Frank,

For many years now the "who invented the mountain bike" story has been written. These stories have typically been written one of two ways:

First; By overworked and underpaid magazine staff members on a tight deadline that gathered recollections from limited sources. Facts went unchecked and many times a sensational "Did not-Did to" slant would be played up.

Second; By any of the bike makers including my company, who were anywhere near Marin in the late seventies or early eighties. The marketing specialists would go to work stretching facts to create cycling gods. The results were never unbiased.

Never did anyone define what invention meant, or what makes a mountain bike a mountain bike.

I had given up hope that the true story would ever be known. After all what did it matter? I am doing well in the industry I love, I am healthy and can still ride a bike. The mountain bike got many adult Americans on bikes for recreation. Now we need to catch up with and pass the rest of the world in integrating the bicycle in a healthier, cleaner transportation solution.
Not to mention my new bike that borrows air bag technology to create wings on demand so cyclists can truly soar with the birds.

Frank, You did the best job by far explaining how the mountain bike got here. Yours is the paper I will give to those wanting to know the story. Would you have taken on this task had you known how difficult it would be to resolve the stories? Do you think it would have been easier if we were all dead?

One aspect of the story I don't think you mentioned was how much fun the development was. The mountain bike was a secret, that once shared, changed people forever. To watch it spread, bringing joy to the world made my contemporaries and I feel like true contributors to society.

Thank you,
 Gary Fisher

Left: Fig. 18.2. The letter from Gary Fisher that was faxed to Frank Berto in response to Frank's paper. The paper's conclusion was that neither Gary nor any other single individual could claim to be the inventor of the mountain bike.

good sense to grant graciously what they could no longer withhold." Gary's letter reminded me of that statement.

By conceding that he didn't invent the mountain bike, Gary has closed the book on the subject. No one will have to write another article. Thank you, Gary.

1968 FUN GARY SUSPENDED FROM RACING FOR LONG HAIR	Left: Fig. 18.3.
1972 FUN GARY TOLD LONG HAIR IS OK	Notwithstanding
FUN **1974** GARY BUILDS THE KLUNKER, THE FIRST-EVER MOUNTAIN BIKE	Gary's admission,
FUN **1977** GARY SETS REPACK RECORD	his company
1979 FUN	catalogs continue
GARY AND PARTNER, CHARLIE KELLY, SELL FIRST-EVER PRODUCTION MOUNTAIN BIKES	to claim that Gary
1983 FUN	invented the
GARY DEVELOPS AND NAMES THE UNICROWN FORK	mountain bike in
1986 FUN	1974.
GARY FOUNDS LARGEST OFF-ROAD RACING TEAM IN THE WORLD	
FUN **1988**	Right: Fig. 18.4.
GARY ENSHRINED IN THE MOUNTAIN BIKE HALL OF FAME	Another catalog
1994 FUN	illustration of the
GARY DUBBED ONE OF THE FOUNDING FATHERS OF MOUNTAIN BIKING	presumed "1974"
1996 FUN	prototype, sporting
GARY BECOMES MASTERS NATIONAL CHAMPION	features that were
FUN **1997**	not available until
GARY INVENTS GENESIS GEOMETRY	much later (such
FUN **1998**	as the Shimano
GARY INTRODUCES THE WORLD TO SUGAR	600 derailleur and
FUN **2002**	the Cook Bros.
GARY GIVES THE WORLD 29ERS— THE NEXT BIG THING	BMX- style fork.
2004 FUN TURN THE PAGE TO FIND OUT	

Bicycle History Déja Vue?

As I was writing my paper for the International Cycle History Conference, I had the eerie feeling that I was walking in the tracks of the historians who covered the inventor of the velocipede more than a century before, and who made such a mess of the record.

I was determined to do better. I'm certainly glad that almost everyone is still alive, because they could correct their recollections when they reviewed the recollections of the others.

After presenting my paper, I asked the conference attendees for their opinions on who invented the mountain bike. Although some felt that my definition of "invent" might be too rigorous, they were unanimous that no one person invented the mountain bike.

THE BIKE THAT MADE HISTORY.
Gary Fisher's 1974 "Clunker"

Chapter 19.
Frank Berto's Repack

The world's original mountain bike race began very casually about ten years ago.* On a Sunday morning, a dozen or so crazies would load their balloon-tired Schwinn clunkers into the back of a pickup truck and drive up the north slope of Marin County's Mount Tamalpais until the truck would go no farther.

From there they pedaled up to the top of what was then called the Cascades fire road, and is now officially called Repack Road.

Notes:

1. This text was first published in the March 1984 issue of *Bicycling!* magazine.

2. At the time the article was first published, the editors of *Bicycling* replaced every occurrence of the term "mountain bike" by "ATB." Here, finally is the "uncensored" version.

Repack Road drops 1,300 feet in 1.8 miles, averaging about a 14 percent grade. Various sections present dirt, gravel, football-size boulders, 20 percent slopes, and rutted, gnarly stretches of bare rock. It made for an exciting, if brief, downhill race.

The early crazies weren't completely mad, so after some preliminary trial runs, they decided that the course was better suited for individual time-trials than for a massed-start race. A pair of stopwatches were used. An official would pedal down the course, stopwatch in pocket, and time the riders as they crossed the finish line.

In the early days, everyone used coaster brakes. By the bottom of the course, the coaster brake would be sizzling hot, with the grease burned out, and it would need to be repacked. That's how the road got its name.

Repack Road also has a good claim to the title of "Birthplace of the Mountain Bike." One crash after another, broken bike by broken bike, the current designs of mountain bikes evolved on the Repack test laboratory.

The race was run fairly regularly through 1979. By then a good Sunday would see as many as 50 bikes, including a few custom-made prototype mountain bikes. Fifteen-speed gear-trains were added so riders could pedal back for a second run. In 1979, Gary Fisher set the record time of 4 minutes, 22 seconds, and Joe Breeze was one second slower.

With the 1979 rainy season, the Repack races ceased. Part of the reason was the increased policing from the Marin Municipal Water District rangers. Outlaw mountain bikers were making nuisances of themselves on the hiking and horse trails. But the main reason was that many of the original organizers had become mountain bike entrepreneurs. Gary Fisher, Charlie Kelly, Joe Breeze, and Erik Koski were spending their weekends designing, building, and selling the prototype MountainBikes, Breezers, and Trailmasters.

I must admit that I watched the development of custom-built clunkers with complete disbelief. I expected mountain bikes to go the way of hula hoops and pet rocks. Clearly, anybody crazy enough to

Right: Fig. 19.1. Going down in flames—or up in smoke? This unidentified rider was not the only one in history to wreck in this curve on Repack. He does have a captive audience, though.

kamikaze down Repack wouldn't have a thousand dollars for a custom-built mountain bike. I didn't believe the movement would survive, until I noticed that every tenth bike in Marin County was an ATB.

Repack is Back

Late last summer, I saw a flier in a bike shop:

"Repack is Back. Competition will be staged on October 8 for a new Repack record; sanctioned by NORBA (National Off-Road Bicycle Association)." I decided to enter. What better way to get on the bandwagon, and besides, someone had to come in last.

I borrowed a Ritchey-Mountain-Bike from Gary Fisher the day before the race. It was an early model, but the gear-train was pure Berto. It had 28/38/48 Shimano Biopace chainrings on 180 mm Sugino Aero Tour cranks. This was combined with a 14-16-18-21-28-38 SunTour New Winner freewheel, a DID chain, and SunTour derailleurs. I switched the brakes from right-hand-front to the conventional pattern. Everything else was stock.

The Rover Boys on Repack

On Saturday morning, I put on my racing uniform: Bell Tourlite helmet, Levi pants and jacket, high boots, and a pair of leather gloves.

I had never pedaled Repack, so I decided to inspect the course before the race. I pedaled the five miles from my home to the finish line in Fairfax, and alternately pedaled and walked up Repack. The bike was geared low enough to climb the 20 percent slopes, but I couldn't convert oatmeal to glycogen fast enough to pedal all the way.

I found that it takes a nice bit of balance to climb steep dirt trails. Lean too far forward and the rear wheel spins; too far back, and the front wheel does a wheelie. I had to climb sitting in the saddle. If I stood up, the front and rear wheels would alternately lose traction. It took me 45 minutes to make it to the top.

The starting line was a typical Mellow Marin mob scene. There were TV crews from two stations, and numerous people with expensive cameras and notebooks. There were also a formidable 60 entrants, with team members from Ross, Specialized Bicycle Imports, and the SE motocross racing team from Los Angeles. Many of the early Repack riders, including Joe Breeze, Otis Guy,

Gary Fisher, and Bob Burrowes, were there to defend their records. Finally, there were these strange bearded characters in jeans and T-shirts, with beer bellies and coaster-brake Goodwill specials. On a 1-to-l0 scale, I was 10 for equipment, 5 for appearance, and 1 for experience.

The race started an hour late. Charlie Kelly, the starter, gave the race invocation: "If you crash and break a few bones, wait for the first-aid crew, unless you're blocking the good line: if so, then try to drag yourself off to one side. If you see somebody down on the course and bleeding, stop and give help unless you're on a real good run. Then, shout at the next first-aid man."

The timer ticked down to zero and the first racer blasted off. I took my camera and walked down to the first "wipe-out" corner. The next rider, Glen Brown (Zzipper Fairings), approached at terminal velocity and slid off the road end-over-end. He got up, inspected himself and his bike for loose pieces, and carried on. I noted that first-aid-

ers and radio hams were stationed about every quarter mile.

The radio at the starting line was alternately reporting crashes and top times. The TV crews headed down the course to where the turkey vultures were circling.

The waiting racers were going through a tire-pinching exercise. The object is to have soft tires for best traction, but not too soft. Pinch-pssst. Pinch-pssst.

A few riders wore shorts, cycling shoes, toe clips, and straps. Think positive.

As the minutes and the riders ticked away. I thought, "Berto,

Right: Fig. 19.2. Another unidentified rider traversing a Repack curve. Poor style, but at least this one has figured out how to stay upright.

aren't you a bit too old for this?"
"But, you've already had your TV interview, so you can't gracefully chicken out."

Five minutes to go. Lower the saddle. Cinch up the helmet. On with the gloves. Set up in middle gear.

"Number 56."

I push up to the starting line.

"Fifteen seconds."

"Five seconds."

"Go!"

Musings Down Repack Road

Push off.

Pedal like crazy down the first 200 yards of level road. Over the edge. First turn approaching. Let's not wipe out on the first corner like Glen Brown.

Get over the rear wheel. Brake! Boy, the front brake really stops, but the rear just skids the back wheel.

Hold your line. Don't hit that gully. Too late! Wham! Crunch! Gosh, nothing broke. Amazing! If this were a skinny-tire bike, it would be in three pieces.

I'm going too slow. Pedal faster.

Gulp! I'll never make this turn. Brake hard! Hold the rear brake on! Slide! What a pounding.

I know the last part is worst. It has those steep, tight corners that slope the wrong way. Here comes the worst curve.

Look at that mob of spectators and they all have cameras. I'm going way too fast. If I'm going to wipe out, let's go down in style.

Lock the rear brake. Right foot down. Slide!

"Go for it, Frank!" shouts a friend. Bump! Bump! Thump! Hang on!

Unreal. I didn't fall. I haven't slid like that since I was 15. Pedal! Pedal! There's the finish line!

Left: Fig. 19.3. The end of the trail, where the bikes get to rest for a while. Note the interesting universal clunker-fixing tool: a pair of vice grips clamped to the seatpost.

At the Finish Line

The timer says "56: 6 minutes, 18 seconds." There are several hundred people at the finish. Slowly, my adrenaline winds down.

The last two riders are the course record holders: Joe Breeze and Gary Fisher. Joe crosses the line in 4 minutes, 44 seconds. Everyone waits for Gary. He crosses the line in 5 minutes, 29 seconds with grease on his white gloves. The chain came off when he skidded into a bush.

The winning times are announced. Two young riders from Roseville, Jim Denton (4:41) and Mike Jordan (4:45), come in first and third. A & B Cycle, their sponsor, will be celebrating. Joe Breeze is second. Ten riders are under 5 minutes. Marcus Gannister of the SBI team is the top novice at 4:58. Denise Caramagno, the editor of *Fat Tire Flyer*, is the top woman at 7:10.

So, the old Repack record still stands. Maybe it's waiting for you. Or, perhaps the new "Over 50 Novice" record of 6:18 is more your style. I'll see you there.

Chapter 20.
Repack Reunion

by Charles Kelly

This had the makings of a great day. Just before hitting the street for Repack, I dug through the old drawer and found the two hand-held digital timers. The last time they were used had been in 1984.

Surely the batteries had turned to green dust by now, more than twelve years later. I popped open the back, and the batteries looked OK. When all else fails, try the on switch. I did, and was rewarded by bright red LED digits. We had precision timing. But only if we wanted it. This was an informal event, a reunion. No one would want to race. The timers were like your old prize ribbons, a link to the past, and only for show. But they worked, and that was nice to know.

I had gotten the word off the street a week or two before the day,

Left: Fig. 20.1. Charlie Kelly in his role as record keeper, starter, and timer, shown here during the 1979 Repack that was recorded by TV station KPIX.

and that was strange. A guy said, "Hey, when's the Repack race?"

It was news to me, but if you knew where to listen, it was all over Fairfax. Repack. Happening. But when? I followed the spoor back to Joe Breeze. He called and asked for phone numbers of guys I hadn't thought about for a long time. I asked, "What's the deal?"

He acted innocent and said, "Yeah, October 21, didn't you realize it? It's the 20th anniversary of the first race. I think some guys are getting together, heading on up there, about 10 in the morning." Something like that.

I was at that race in October 1976, and Joe wasn't. I wouldn't have known that date, but Joe had made a thesis out of something we did only 24 times in our lives. No fact is too obscure. He has mined my battered notebooks that hold all the known race results, and built a database that can tell you the day anyone made his or her best run. And though I didn't have any idea what the date of the first race was, I knew Joe was close. Twenty years this October.

When I heard this, I knew I would not want to be anywhere on the planet on October 21, 1996 at 10:00 AM except the top of Repack.

I kept running into old friends that morning, cruising the streets on their old bikes, and it took a while to get out of town. I got so far behind schedule that I accepted a pickup truck ride to the top of the paved road. A ride up the hill was more important when the bikes weighed twice as much and had one gear, but being behind schedule was a convenient excuse to avoid half the climbing. We parked at the top of Azalea Hill, and a few more carloads showed up. I knew some of the riders getting out, and they had some old iron to ride, so they showed it off, one-speed with a coaster brake and no front brake, a bike that will not stop on this course in less than a couple of hundred feet, which is about twice as far as you can see most of the time.

Guys started orbiting slowly, watching others putting wheels on and getting bikes off racks. I didn't know what the delay was, but when I got tired of waiting for anyone to move toward the dirt road, I took off, and they all followed me. Hmmm. I hope they don't think I'm in charge of this.

Riding slowly up the last part of the approach, I saw a scene from photos taken long ago. The autumn lighting was the same: low morning sun slanting across a perfectly clear blue sky on a cool fall morning. A time capsule opened in front of me.

Instead of the rainbow of bright jerseys and company logos you see at any typical mountain bike event, I saw a single orange Lycra jersey adrift in a sea of blue denim. How did a guy who dresses like that even hear about it? Shorts? Helmets? Out of the question. Levis, boots, work shirt, and baseball cap are what you wear to race Repack. If there was a jersey, the only appropriate one was Velo-Club Tamalpais, muted blue and yellow without a dozen manufacturer's logos, worn over a pair of jeans. I see that Ross Parkerson's VCT jersey is worn only for ceremonial occasions now, because it is held together by little more than hope.

About half the assembly of about 60 riders were on the latest high-tech machinery, and that was only because they no longer had their old bikes. The other half was on the largest collection of retro, original, carefully hoarded, obsolete iron that has ever been assembled, much less raced, in about two decades. There were no in-between bikes. No 1985 Stumpjumpers. It was either primitive, pre-1940 iron with Texas "longhorn" handlebars or new $3,000 Y-frame full-suspension 19-pound carbon fiber machinery. On half-a-dozen old bikes was the classic clunker tool kit, a pair of Vise-Grips clamped to the seatpost. This took the place of socket sets and screwdrivers for creative trail repairs, and provided its own way to attach to the bike.

Otis Guy and Joe Breeze brought their original bikes, a pair of Schwinns with coaster brakes, fork braces, steel rims, original

Above and right: Figs. 20.2 & 20.3. Some ride their bikes up Pine Mountain Road under their own steam, while others haul them up in a pickup truck.

paint, and Uniroyal tires. Otis has a Morrow, the most desirable possible downhill brake, and Joe has the lever-shifted Bendix two-speed. Craig Weichel rode his Pro-Cruiser with no front brake, and Alan Bonds showed up on a perfect specimen of a circa 1976 Schwinn conversion, with a new "Excelsior" spear-point paint job, drum brakes front and rear, and perfect Brooks B-72 saddle.

At the other end of the scale, Gary Fisher arrived on a Y-frame Fisher, but suitably attired in jeans, while I had my Ritchey P-21 and I wore the jeans and U.S. Army fatigue shirt that are not only what I wore then, but what I have worn most every day since. I would have ridden the old iron if I still had it, but the only one I didn't ride into the ground is in the museum in Crested Butte now.

Because only 200 people ever got to race Repack, it's just something to read about, like reading about climbing Mount Everest, and its importance is questionable for anyone who was never there. It was important to me; and several major

mountain bike developers still refer to it as some big deal, which keeps the image alive. Repack changed every part of my life, and it's an era that was so fleeting and so much fun that I've spent a lot of time since then trying to capture it in print.

Repack wasn't the first place anyone raced downhill. There were other guys in Marin having races as early as 1969, and it wouldn't surprise me if it happened in a lot of places. So why do all these elitist guys who got to be there claim that it was such a big deal?

First, Repack is hard enough to ride that riding it at all was originally a challenge for coaster-brake riders with far less experience than anyone has now. Ten minutes on Repack was the most condensed lesson in off-road riding you could get

Right: Fig. 20.4. Charlie Kelly at work descending Repack in the good old days—knee pads and all (though no helmet)—riding his original Breezer.

in 1976, and you either learned fast or took up tennis instead. A coaster brake will not stop you on a steep hill but will barely slow you down. You have to start the turn long before you get to it, and you have to get the bike sideways for a while before it grudgingly changes direction. There is no comparison with a light modern bike with great brakes and suspension. A coaster brake requires commitment—top to bottom, blind turns whatever -because you're gonna ram anything that gets in the way. There was a good reason most people in the 1970s thought we were crazy.

A coaster brake turns kinetic energy into heat, and it keeps it all in a small place. Repack will heat the hub far beyond whatever it is rated to handle. If you don't have a front brake, the coaster brake will be

Fig. 20.5. Two generations of mountain bikes: "old iron" and a suspension bike.

smoking at the bottom, and if you were dumb enough to ride with a New Departure instead of a Morrow or a Bendix or even a Musselman brake, that bogus brake would be ground to dust halfway down and you would be in free-fall.

On that morning in 1976, some of us got together to settle once and for all who was the fastest downhiller on dirt. We decided we would do it as a time-trial, to give everyone the same chance, and that may have been the breakthrough that made the race so popular.

It required far more organization to pull off a race like that than just getting a few people together at the top of the hill and yelling, "Go!" We didn't have radio contact between the start and finish lines, so timing had to be done carefully. We started with a Navy chronometer and an alarm clock with sweep second hand, but within a few weeks of the first race, Fred Wolf and I had each spent $70 to purchase a matched pair of the first digital stopwatches to hit the market. Times given in hundredths of a second give riders confidence that the results are accurately measured, and even if the confidence was only as good as the timers' handling of the clocks, there were no ties and no arguments. No one was so critical of the timing system that they wanted to do it themselves, and it fell to me to handle the timing and keep the records in a beat-up notebook that now has sweat stains on a lot of the pages.

Repack created a standard that no other form of racing could. How long will it take you to get down the hairiest hill we could find? The standard to shoot at was 5 minutes. If you could get under that time, you joined the top 10 percent, about 20 riders: you were an Expert, and you raced against Experts. Until you broke five minutes, you raced in the Novice class.

The field grew slowly over the first three years to about 30 riders who could be counted on to show up, and 5 or 10 more who might. The race felt like it was as fair as anyone could expect it to be. Because the riders started at 2-minute intervals in inverse order of their best times, the times would usually get faster with each new rider to arrive at the finish over a period of about an hour. Years later, I saw that it often took hours at supposedly organized events to sort out winners, but at Repack, with only a paper system and two timers, no radios and no computers, we gave complete results with any number of riders, in two racing categories, a

couple of minutes after the last rider finished.

Far from answering anything with our first race, it turned out that we asked the eternal question, and the answer changed daily. In the first race, Alan Bonds was the only rider who got all the way down without a crash, and it was the winning strategy. It was important to go fast, but it was more important to stay on the bike. That didn't sit right with guys who had figured they would win and then would never have to defend the title. No one had figured he was going to crash, but there's a difference between just riding the hill and racing the hill. OK, Alan, you got lucky. Think you'll be lucky in a week? Be here.

That's how it started. Everyone wanted a shot at the title. Joe Breeze showed up from Mill Valley for the

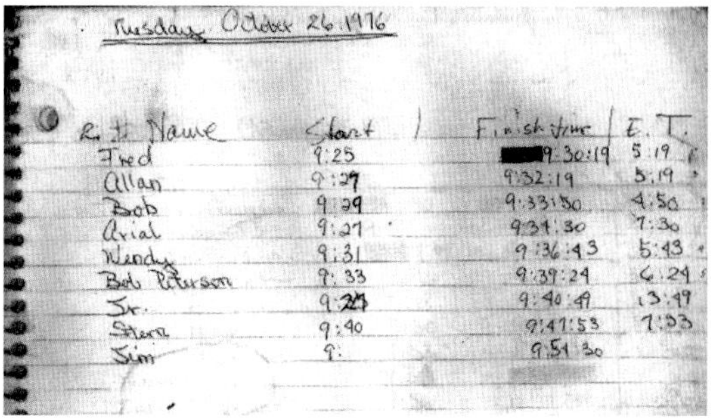

Fig. 20.6. The first recorded Repack results—for Repack No. 2—as entered in Charlie Kelly's Repack notebook.

third race, along with some of the Larkspur guys who called themselves the Canyon Gang, riders who shredded their side of the mountain and had been at it longer than we had. Gary Fisher raced in the fifth event. After that the word got to the riders from the Berkeley Trailers Union (BTU) across the bay, guys remarkably like us in their equipment and attitudes, and the arms race was on. The race was so hard on equipment that just having a bike that would go the distance was an advantage, where the attrition rate was over half of the riders either crashing or damaging their bikes.

Even though some of the races were won by coaster-brake riders, the repairs that were necessary afterward and gave the hill its name made it a hassle for all but the most dedicated kickback people. Front and rear drum brakes had become the choice by 1976 because they allowed for gears and hand-operated brakes on the bike. Amazingly, the coaster-brake group included Joe Breeze, who won the most events, until he had made his own frame in 1977. Part of the impetus for building that frame was my pressure on him to make a bike for me that would give me a competitive advantage that my modest skills didn't. Joe did, but he kept the first one,

and by the time he had finished his own bike, there were eight more people who wanted one of those bikes. Hardly anyone ever asks me, but if I had to pick the day mountain biking started, it was the day in September 1977 that Joe rolled out his first Breezer, inspired by Repack.

Aside from creating a need for improved equipment and a place to test it, Repack did one more thing that made it important to mountain biking, and it was something that people noticed. The organized but informal underground competition was wacky and harmless, and "Very California.' It surfaced in "Clunker Bikes," an article in the Spring 1978 "CoEvolution Quarterly" that mentioned the Repack race and a place in Colorado called Crested Butte as the homes of the sport. A year later I made my first writing sale, to *Bicycling*, with a story about Repack, and followed with another on mountain biking in a national outdoor magazine, and suddenly I had another career. I wrote for magazines. The only thing I was expert enough to write about was mountain bikes, and because hardly anyone else knew enough to write about them, I found that I could keep selling articles.

In 1979 a camera crew from a San Francisco TV station talked me

Chapter 20. Repack Reunion

into putting on a race for them to film. It didn't take much reason to do a race, and that was as good as any, and we had a great turnout. The film had everything, including Matthew Seiler's bike sailing directly over the cameraman's head, and a long-haired rider diving down a bank to retrieve it, remounting, straightening his bars and riding off. Interviews with riders still pumping adrenaline were wide-eyed, hyperventilated and funny. The piece was broadcast locally, then later on a national program, and the old footage is a priceless documentary of "A Day in the Life." Mountain bikes had been noticed, and Repack was the reason.

Back to the hill, present time. I pulled out the timers, and no one seemed surprised that I had brought them or that they worked. It was as though I was expected to bring them. Each timer had a 20-year-old bottle cap taped over the reset switch to prevent accidents. Once the clocks were started (by banging together the start buttons), they could not be shut off or reset without removing the tape.

It was time for me to get out of there and beat the rush. Riding the hill that changed my life, and by extension a lot of other lives, is a spiritual experience for me. I don't go there that often, probably two or three times a year now, even though it is within five miles of my house, but you never forget the road, and I don't have any problem knowing what is around every turn. All the longtime riders have it memorized, because knowing every rock and rut and the radius of blind turns was a cheaper advantage than technology. People worked hard to memorize it. One day I walked down from the top with a friend who took a photograph every 50 feet, converting the results to slides that we could pro-

Fig. 20.7. That's not a spill, just another way of making it through that nasty curve.

ject in sequence as a memory aid. Joe made detailed maps, with all landmarks noted, for his own study.

The number of regulars who ride here is enough that the "groove" is easily visible, six inches wide, polished of loose rocks that are everywhere else on the road, and snaking from side to side across the ruts. When bicycle suspension systems arrived on Repack, the charac-

Fig. 20.8. Alan Bonds coming down on one of his beautifully restored derailleur clunkers.

ter of the braking ripples into the switchbacks changed. The distance between ripples went from a couple of inches to a foot or so. I usually follow the groove on the road, but Joe says it's wrong in a lot of places, and he is as good an authority as anyone, with the second-fastest time recorded. One thing about Repack, you never have any idea how anyone else does it. All you can know is how you do it, and you wonder how anyone can do it so much faster.

I guess people use the word "technical" now to mean gnarly. Even with modern brakes and suspension, you can't stop on the steepest part, a stretch of loose gravel and deep dust scattered over what feels like a cliff about 50 yards long near the top. Your best hope is to control your out-of-controlness and try to drift under maximum braking to the right part of the off-camber surface, to line up with the road when it opens up and you can let go of the brakes, so your tires suddenly get traction back, and you accelerate so fast you can feel the G-forces slapping you in the back. Gotta ride in the weeds on the left side of the road on the next turn, stay out of the parallel ruts in the middle. How did I ever do this with just a coaster brake?

I had only one really bad crash on Repack. Nothing in my life ever hit me as hard as this road hit me in the chest, right here at the steepest part, on a fall day in 1979. I was so stunned that I had no idea if I was all right and just couldn't feel anything—or dying. I lay there without moving for a minute or so, because I wanted to put off finding out how injured I really was. At a Repack race you didn't see anyone for most of the length of the course, because people only gathered at the bottom, and the top had no one. There was no sympathy anywhere to be found.

I thought, Bob Burrowes would be getting off the starting line in about 30 seconds, and when he came around that curve he would ride between my legs at 35 miles per hour, and he would not be happy if I spoiled his run by causing him to crash. It was not a good time or place to lie in the road. I found that I could move, and that the skateboarder's gloves, knee pads, and elbow pads had kept me from being battered at the contact points. I was more alive than I had ever been. I heard the sound of Repack, Bob's tires ricocheting off the rocks above me, and grunts when he scared himself. I dragged my bike to the side in time for him to rocket past with a good line.

You hated to crash and spoil someone else's run, because if you did, you were going to hear about it from the other rider. No one got a lot of shots at the Repack title, and it was an effort just to get to the start. Wasting a run because of another rider's mistake was the worst thing that could happen, and you would have to look pretty badly injured before another racer would blow his run by stopping to help you.

I think these thoughts in the two seconds it takes to pass the spot. Repack is fast and slow at the same time. It's like listening to your favorite song. You know exactly what is going to happen.

Halfway down I see trucks on the road, and I slow down to touring speed. The rangers are nice enough to be where you can see them a long way off. It doesn't matter if I go by slowly, and it feels good that it doesn't. I can cruise past these guys, and as soon as I get around the turn, I'm gone.

I don't miss the old equipment. If there is one thing you remember from a 50-pound bike with drum brakes, it is the grip it took to operate the brakes. Drum brakes fade as they heat up, and as you went down Repack, it took more and more grip on the longest motorcycle levers you could get. By the time you got to the bottom you had to practically pry your fingers off the handlebars. It was painful during the ride, and for the next half hour your forearms would burn from the effort.

Joe Breeze has named every part of Repack. There's Yellow Face, Upper and Lower Dipper, Danger X, and so on. Here's the spot we call "Vendetti's Face." Marc Vendetti went down there in the second or third Repack, and he left a good portion of his face on the road. We knew something was wrong, because his time was too long. Anyone who wasn't down in 5 minutes was not having a good run. If it was over 6, you knew there was trouble, but no one cared to trudge up the hill to see what it was unless it went up to an hour or so. Marc arrived at the finish stunned, blood running down his face, and Ray Flores caught it on film. It was classic, I tell ya.

Through the switchbacks, then Camera Corner, a hard left that is featured in all the old photo collec-

tions. Over the off-camber rock that years ago Alan Bonds and I spent an afternoon attacking with a pick to see if we could create a better line on the turn. It's a hard rock, and even the road grader that scrapes the road every couple of years has given up, as we did. The hump remains, and I have the same thought I always had when I went over it: if you could cut just a little channel through the left side of the rock, you could line up on this corner perfectly and take 2 seconds off your time. I was talking with Joe Breeze, and we commiserated that there is no good way to get over this rock and set up for the turn. It always feels as though you did it wrong, and if there's a right way you can just never find it.

When I got to the bottom, I was one of the first there. The racers were waiting for casuals like me to clear the course, and Joe Breeze had mentioned while we were at the top that he had stashed a couple of kegs of beer at the bottom, which got things rolling. By the time the first racers got down the hill, there was a party going on.

The Repack finish line is a lonely rock that sticks up out of a

Fig. 20.9. Charlie Kelly going down full blast in a cloud of Repack dust.

level piece of ground, a rough, dome-shaped monument about 3 feet high, about 3 feet across, and uncomfortable as hell to sit on. It has no name: it's just the rock. I have spent a lot of time sitting on it writing race results while the sharp angles stabbed my butt, and standing on top of it addressing small gatherings of people like the one I'm looking at today.

The finish is not a straightway: it's a blind left turn to the rock that marks the actual line, and you can't see the rock until you are about 30 feet from it. Everyone tries a flashy sideways stop. If you didn't try to finish sideways, everyone would say, "What's wrong with him?" So everyone is out of control at the finish, because the turn tightens up, and the rock is a good perch, because when the sideways riders hit it, it doesn't move.

A couple of the old bikes come in with coaster brakes in the classic condition, a stinking cloud of petroleum smoke pouring off the hub, burned grease running down the spokes, and the hub shell so hot that someone always spits on it to see it boil away and hear the sizzle.

The party around the rock is like old times—so many conversations going on at once that it sounds like a schoolyard during recess, a "bike pile" growing as riders fling one-speeds on top to show how much they don't worry about 50 pounds of indestructible iron that has been stripped of anything nonessential. After some calculation by Chris on his envelope, the winners are announced. They high-five each other, and that is that. We've used it all up, whatever it was. The beer runs out and people start to drift off.

I don't know when the next event will be, but I never knew that in 1979 either. When the sun and moon and stars line up, it will happen.

Fig. 20.10. The 1996 Repack Reunion line-up. Second from the right is Scott Petersen, who has gained some pounds but, now in his 70s, is still kicking butt.

Chapter 21.
Where Are They Now?

Most of the mountain bike pioneers were quite young at the time, and it may be of interest to find out how they're doing now. Just fine, thank you, for most of them. The following sections will give you an idea of their personal and professional developments since the early days of the mountain bike.

Gary Fisher

These days, Gary Fisher lives in San Francisco, having just moved there from Marin County, where he had lived most of his life. He is President of Gary Fisher Bicycles, a division of Trek Bicycle Corporation. Now in his late 50s, he is still doing what he loves most: racing bikes on- and off-road. With his flamboyant persona, he has continued to inspire others to ride.

He has also made several technical contributions to mountain bike development. In 1982 he introduced

Left: Fig. 21.1. Gary Fisher loves to stand out in a crowd.

Right: Fig. 21.2. A modern Gary Fisher bike with 29-inch wheels.

oversize headsets, which made for more predictable steering and handling. In recent years, Gary has pioneered the use of larger-diameter (29-inch) wheels for larger-size mountain bikes.

Joe Breeze

Today, Joe lives in Fairfax and heads his own company, Breezer Bikes, which designs and markets a full line of "city bikes," i.e. bicycles that can actually be used to transport people and goods, rather than just as toys.

In the early 1980s, Joe, together with Josh Angell, designed and marketed the "Hite-Rite," an ingenious spring-loaded device for raising and lowering the seat height "on the fly." Today's mountain bikes don't seen to ask for seat height adjustments, so the market for such devices has dried up, but it was quite a cash cow while it lasted.

Joe continues to be very committed to popularizing "practical" cycling, and he was one of the founding members of the Marin County Bicycle Coalition, a bicycle advocacy group.

Charlie Kelly

Today, Charlie lives in San Anselmo and operates a piano moving business. He is still the keeper of the sacred records of early mountain biking. He runs a piano-moving business in Marin County, and still writes about mountain biking for various bicycle magazines. Although he uses a van to move pianos, he relies almost exclusively on his bicycle for his everyday transportation needs.

Tom Ritchey

Today, Tom lives in La Honda, California, and owns his own company, Ritchey Designs, producing well-engineered bicycle components. The company had been selling bicycles,

Left: Fig. 21.3. Joe Breeze today.

Below: Fig. 21.4. An example of the type of bikes now sold by Joe Breeze.

both road and mountain bikes, until 1999.

He is now actively involved in Project Rwanda, which provides "coffee bikes" for Rwandan small farmers to transport their harvest of coffee cherries to the drying plants. Over 1,000 of these bikes designed by Tom and built in Taiwan are currently in use by Rwandan farmers.

And What Happened to the Mountain Bike?

Since its timid beginnings, the mountain bike has become the most common bicycle around, at least in the U.S. Today, most adult bicycles sold are either mountain bikes or something that looks like a mountain bike—flat handlebars, fat tires, derailleur gearing and all.

But the development of the mountain bike did not stop once it became publicly accepted around

1983. Perhaps the most significant development has been the introduction and proliferation of suspension systems. Although individuals had been tinkering with front and rear suspension before, the breakthrough came in 1989 when motorcycle suspension expert Paul Turner introduced the first RockShox suspension fork for mountain bike use.

After that, only a few years went by before several manufacturers included suspension forks as standard equipment on many of their bikes. And it wasn't too long before numerous ideas for rear suspension were developed and eagerly adopted.

Other components also went through significant development. Mountain bike derailleur gearing grew from 15 to 18, to 21, 24, and now 27-speed gearing. And the gear

Above: Fig. 21.5. Tom Ritchey still handles the blow torch at times.

Left: Fig. 21.6. A Ritchey-designed Rwanda "coffee bike."

selection process has been eased by indexed gearing as well as developments in the shift levers and tooth patterns. But the most curious development of recent years is the "single-speed": a mountain bike stripped off its derailleur gearing. That seems like a return to the clunker from which the mountain bike was hatched in the first place (but now without the weight and with good brakes).

Another component that has undergone quite some change is the braking system. The first mountain bikes invariably came with cantilever brakes. Later, also U-brakes and cam-actuated brakes were tried. Then suddenly "everybody," including Shimano stumbled upon the old principle of the direct-pull brake (also called V-brake). More recently disk brakes became popular. They do work better under wet conditions than rim brakes, but they are also more sensitive and trouble-prone.

That, perhaps is the major change in mountain bike design over the years: They've become more sophisticated, and consequently also more sensitive. If you've ever tried "tuning" a full-suspension bike, you may find yourself wistfully longing back for those early bomber bikes...

Above: Fig. 21.7. The 2008 Specialized Stumpjumper FSR Elite is a modern full-suspension cross-country trails bike.

Top right: Fig. 21.8. The 2008 Schwinn Frontier is a basic hardtail trail-riding bike.

Bottom right: Fig. 21.9. The 2008 GT DHI Pro is a downhill or "Freeride" bike.

Annotated Bibliography

1. May 1930. *CTC Gazette*. "Some Weights and a Specification," by Vernon Blake. Describes his geared, cantilever-braked fat-tire bicycle for bad roads.

2. 1962 Schwinn catalog. Shows the Schwinn Corvette.

3. August 1974. *Popular Science*. "Moto-Bike: Off-Road Bicycle Built Like a Motorcycle." Describes the 1974 Yamaha one-speed coaster- brake Moto-Bike with front and rear suspension.

4. May 30, 1977. Working drawing for the frame of Joe Breeze's first Breezer. This was the first modern mountain bike to be produced in quantity (ten).

5. February 1, 1978. *VeloNews*. "California Bikies are 'Mountainside Surfing'" by Owen Mulholland. This is the earliest published article on Marin mountain biking that I have. Mulholland describes the first meeting between Gary Fisher and Charlie Kelly and says, "Gary mentioned the bike parts warehouse he occasionally also referred to as "home," and pretty soon the two were hard at work on some heavy modifications. First came a front drum brake, then ten speeds with the usual alloy crank setup, then 25-year-old Schwinn cantilever brakes, a Brooks B-72 saddle, and finally the logical outcome of such a line of development, their own frames, these being made by local master craftsman Joe Breeze." This sounds like a description of Charlie Kelly's first Breezer.

6. Spring 1978. *CoEvolution Quarterly*. "Clunker Bikes," by Richard Nilsen. Describes the early developments of mountain bikes in Marin. Describes the first Breezers. Says, "A revolutionary moment in this history occurred three or four years ago when Gary Fisher got the idea of putting a ten-speed derailleur assembly on a balloon-tired bicycle."

7. September 29, 1978. *Crested Butte Chronicle* and *Crested Butte Pilot*. Describes the (second or third) Crested Butte to Aspen event.

8. October 8,1978. *The Washington Post*. "New California Fad Clunker Bikes." I don't have this reference.

9. October 29, 1978. Charlie Kelly's flyer for the 18th Repack Race. The poster is drawn by Pete Barrett.

10. January 1979. *Bicycling*. "Clunkers Among the Hills," by Charles R. Kelly. Describes the Repack race. Pictures of a Breezer.

11. September 1979. *Mariah Outside*. "Built To Take It," by Charles R. Kelly. This article was first written in 1977, rejected, and rewritten several times before it was finally published in 1979. Describes the evolution of the mountain bike from the Canyon Gang to Velo- Club Tamalpais, from Repack to Crested Butte, and from clunkers to Breezers.

    On the first page, there is an interesting picture by Wende Cragg of a mud-covered bike. Gary Fisher recalls that this is the ten-speed bike he built for Fred Wolf at about the same time that he built his own first derailleur clunker "prototype." The picture shows a drum brake, a five-speed freewheel, an Ashtabula 50-36 double crankset, and 1974-75 vintage SunTour derailleurs. Charlie Kelly says, "The problem was solved when one rider discovered that tandem bicycles had drum rear brakes as well as a five-speed gear cluster. A little tinkering, and filing, and a derailleur was mounted on an old ballooner."

12. November 27, 1979. Letter from Charlie Kelly to Russ Mahon on MountainBikes letterhead. Says, "I watched the Mill Valley cyclo-cross in '74 and was blown out by the ballooner action. Please send me a spec. list of the bikes in use. These were the first multi-speed ballooners I ever saw, and we jumped on the concept hard at about the same time. You can see how hard we jumped on it." This letter is reproduced on page XXX.

13. December 1979. *City Sports*. "Working Up an Appetite." by Darryl Skrabak, describing the dirty fun of the Thanksgiving "Appetite Seminars" put on by Charlie Kelly.

14. January 1980. *Bicycle Motocross Action.* "Full Bore Cruisers." Interviews with Mert Lawill, Gary Fisher, Charlie Kelly, and Joe Breeze. Situation in Marin at the end of 1979. Consensus of the four makers was that clunkers should be called mountain bikes.

15. February 1980. BMX Plus. "The Ritchey Mountain Bike Test."

16. April 1980. *Bicycling.* "Rocky Mountain High," by Charles R. Kelly. Describes the 4th Crested Butte to Aspen Clunker Tour.

17. May 1980. *Bicycle Dealer Showcase.* "Mountain Biking: Off-Road to Happiness." I don't have this reference.

18. Mid-1980. MountainBikes catalog. This is my earliest catalog. Lists Uniroyal knobby tires.

19. July 25, 1980. *Pacific Sun.* "Clunker Capital of the World," by Richard Street. Interviews with Gary Fisher and Charlie Kelly. Status in Marin in 1980.

20. August/September 1980. *Fat Tire Flyer.* Issue One. The *FTF* was published quarterly originally with Charlie Kelly as editor and publisher (later with Denise Caramagno as publisher). The *FTF* was the voice of the mountain bike for the next eight years.

21. Fall 1980. MountainBikes catalog. Details of the first Ritchey frame and the components used in 1980. Lists Mitsuboshi skinwall tires. Details and picture of John Finley Scott's 1953 "Woodsy Bike."

22. January 1981. *City Sports.* "Klunking Away." Describes the November 1980 District Cyclo-Cross Championship in Sacramento. Gary Fisher came second on a mountain bike.

23. 1981. MountainBikes catalog. Details of the 1981 bikes. Brief biographies of Charlie Kelly, Gary Fisher, and Tom Ritchey. Gary's biography says, "In seven years of off-road bicycle experimentation, he has pioneered the use of multiple gearing on balloon-tire bikes and the use of motorcycle parts for dirt riding." It did not say that Gary invented the mountain bike.

24. May 1981. *Bicycling.* "Buying an Off-Road Touring Bike," by John Schubert. Describes the differences between BMX bikes, cruisers, and off-road touring bikes. Bicycling just would not call them mountain bikes.

25. May 1981. *Bicycle Dealer Showcase.* "A Bike for All Seasons," by John Francis. Status of the 1981 Market. Pictures of the 1980 Ritchey-MountainBikes, Breeze Breezer, S & S Big Foot, CW Racing, Jeff Lindsay Mountain Goat, and Murray Baja bikes.

26. July 1981. *City Sports.* "A Rebirth For Big Bikes," by Darryl Skrabak. Describes the transition from 1950s roadsters to 1960s three-speeds to 1970s ten-speeds to clunkers. Gives reasons for the changes. Says, "Gary Fisher is credited with first adaptation of derailleur gearing to an off-road bike."

27. July 1981. *American Bicyclist and Motorcyclist.* "Mountain Bikes: A Different Breed," by Charles R. Kelly. Says, "Gary Fisher, now of MountainBikes, turned his old Schwinn Excelsior into a five-speed by bolting on a tandem drum brake. After he added thumb-shifters, a quick-release seatpost, and motorcycle brake levers, the rush was on."

28. 1982. Specialized catalog. Shows the 1982 Specialized Stumpjumper.

29. 1982. Univega catalog. Shows the 1982 Univega Alpina Sport.

30. 1982. MountainBikes catalog. Details of the Ritchey frame and the components used in 1982.

31. 1982. Schwinn catalog. Shows the 1982 King Sting and Sidewinder.

32. May 1982. *The Fiat Tyre.* Newsletter of Western Wheelers. Interviews with Mike Sinyard and Tom Ritchey.

33. May 1982. *Bicycle Dealer Showcase.* "The Future Now?" By John Francis. Status of the 1982 Market.

34. May 1982. *Bicycling.* "A Look at the Long Beach Bike Show," by Frank Berto. I counted 20 fat-tire bikes.

35. June 1982. *Bicycling.* "The Klunkers of Marin," by John Schubert. Road Test of three different models of Ritchey MountainBikes, Koski Trailmaster, Breeze Breezer, Lindsay

Mountain Goat, and Specialized Stumpjumper. Schubert says, "In the mid-1970s, he (Fisher) was the first on his block to add five-speed derailleur gearing to his newspaper-boy-style clunker."

36. October 1982. *Bike Tech*. "The View from Japan" by Gary Fisher. Describes Gary Fisher's and Tom Ritchey's trip to Japan and how the Japanese companies jumped aboard the mountain bike trend.

37. 1983. Specialized catalog. Shows the Stumpjumper and Stumpjumper Sport.

38. March 1983. Kelly-Fisher MountainBikes catalog. The first catalog issued after the break-up with Tom Ritchey.

39. March/April 1983. *Fat Tire Flyer*. Lists 22 makers of mountain bikes selling for more than $600. Had an article by Frank Berto on mountain bike gearing. The write-up for Kelly-Fisher MountainBikes says, "The Legendary Gary Fisher is the first mountain biker in history to have taken the fenders and coaster brakes off his old newspaper boy clunker bike to put on derailleurs in the early 1970s."

40. Spring 1983. *Bicycling News Canada*. "Ritchey Mountain Bike (Japanese Version)." Road Test of the Montare.

41. May 1983. *Bicycling*. "Off-Road Test: Fat Tires Come of Age," by John Schubert. Road Test of six ATBs.

42. July 1983. *City Sports*. "The New Trend in Treads," by Laurence Malone.

43. December 1983. *Bicycling*. "All-Terrain Bike Test Ballooner Bonanza," by John Schubert. Road Test of eight ATBs.

44. Winter 1983. *Sun Tour Inside Line*. "Mountain Bike Special." Articles by Erik Koski and Chris Allen. Bibliography of early articles on fat-tire bikes.

45. September? 1984. *Marin Independent Journal*. Article by Beth Ashley. Interviews with Gary Fisher, Jeff Bedford, and Charlie Kelly.

46. 1984. Specialized catalog. Shows the 1984 Stumpjumper.

47. 1984. Fisher MountainBikes catalog. Shows the Montare, Mt. Tam, Everest 84, and Competition MountainBikes.

48. March 1984. *Bicycling*. "Repack Revisited," by Frank Berto. Discussion of the early Repack races. Impressions of the course. Frank Berto's time: 6 minutes, 18 seconds. [Editor's note: This article is reprinted in this volume as Chapter 16, "Frank's Repack."]

49. April 1984. *Mariah Outside*. "Fat is Back," by Craig Vetter. Says Gary Fisher added gears in 1974.

50. 1984. *The Mountain Bike Book*. By Rob Van der Plas. This was the first mountain bike book, and Rob did some original research. Rob says that Gary Fisher modified his Schwinn to take derailleur gearing.

51. March 1985. *Bicycling*. "The Vanguard," by Charlie Kelly. Interviews with Gary Fisher, Joe Breeze, Tom Ritchey, Steve Potts, and Charlie Cunningham. Says, "Fisher is credited with being the first Marin County rider to put gears on his 'clunker.' Others had done similar variations as early as 1953, hut Fisher's innovation of gears on a fat-tire bike is credited with being the lineal ancestor of the modern mountain machine."

52. September 1987. *Mountain Bike Action*. "Inside the Pros' Bikes." Picture and description of Gary Fisher's Excelsior clunker. Write-up says this bike was racing down Mount Tamalpais in the summer of 1976, and notes that the Shimano 600 derailleur is 1976 vintage.

53. 1988. *Richard's Mountain Bike Book*. By Charles Kelly and Nick Crane. This book contains the best history of the mountain bike. Charlie Kelly wrote, "Although Gary Fisher is generally credited with being the first person to try a drum brake five-speed hub on his clunker, he should more properly he credited with being the first person in Marin County to do so."

54. 1991. *Climb Every Mountain the Mountain Bike Way*. By Andy Bull. Andy tells the mountain bike history, as told to him in 1991 by Gary Fisher. The best part of the book is the picture of Gary Fisher doing a fake wheelie on a green Schwinn Excelsior clunker. This 1975 derailleur clunker is

closer to the first mountain bike than Gary's "1974 prototype". It has an Ashtabula front fork, Ashtabula double crankset, front and rear drum brakes, and motorcycle brake levers. The Shimano Positron stem-shifters (the model with two cables to the rear derailleur) mounted on the handlebars date this bike to at least mid-1975.

55. September 1991. *Marin Independent Journal*. Article by Beth Ashley. "Mario's Mountain Bikes Sweep the World."

56. December 1991. *Interbike Buyer*. "The Pioneers of Mountain Biking," by Charles Kelly. Describes mountain biking in Marin in the 1970s.

57. July, 1992. *Japan Cycle Press*. Interviews with Tom Ritchey, Ritchey Design; Gary Fisher, Gary Fisher Bicycles; and Ross Shafer, Salsa Cycles. The Fisher article says, "In 1974 he built his first mountain bike for his own pleasure and found that people who tried it loved it."

58. June 1994. *Smithsonian*. "Over Hill, Over Dale, on a Bicycle Built for Goo," by Donald M. Schwartz. Interviews with Gary Fisher and Charlie Kelly. Describes the current state of mountain biking.

59. 1995. *Mountain Bike Almanac*. By Grant Wolf Inc. This book is a trove of mountain bike history and statistics. It includes articles by Joe Breeze, Gary Fisher, and Charlie Kelly. Joe Breeze's article on mountain bike origins starts with the statement, "There were many steps in the evolution of the mountain bike. There was no single inventor." Gary Fisher ends his article saying, "In 1974, I blacksmithed the now famous clunker from scavenged objects."

60. 1996. *No Hands*. By Judith Crown and Glenn Coleman. This book presents the history of the Schwinn Bicycle Company. Chapter 9 is the mountain bike story based on interviews with Gary Fisher, Charlie Kelly, Joe Breeze, Tom Ritchey, and Mike Sinyard. The basic facts are reasonably accurate.

61. March 1996. *Bicycling*. "Who Really Invented the Mountain Bike?" By Joe Breeze. Describes the December 1, 1974 Mill Valley cyclo-cross race and Russ Mahon's bikes. Says there was no single inventor.

62. June 1996. *Bicycling*. Letters to the Editor. Gary Fisher says, "I built my 18-speed clunker in September of '74, not summer '75." Breeze responds, "Fisher did not have derailleurs on his bike in December 1974."

63. August 6, 1996. *Marin Independent Journal*. "Different Spokes —Who Really Invented the Mountain Bike?" Article by Richard Polito. Interviews with Gary Fisher, Joe Breeze, Charlie Kelly, and Tom Ritchey. Tom Ritchey recalls that Gary Fisher said, "Tom, the person who invented the mountain bike is the person with the biggest printing press."

64. October 24, 1996. *Marin Independent Journal*. "Fat Tire Faithful Return to Repack." Article by Richard Polito. Describes the 1996 Repack Reunion.

65. September 1, 1997. *Bicycle Retailer and Industry News*. "Joe Breeze Celebrates 20 Years of Innovation." History of Joe Breeze's mountain bike innovations.

66. September 1997. *Mountain Biker*. "A Brief History of Mountain Bike Time." Lists the significant dates including the 1974 Mill Valley cyclo-cross race. Does not mention Gary Fisher's September 1974 date.

67. April 5, 1997. *St. Louis Post Dispatch*. Article by Ralph Loos. Claims that mountain bikes were invented in Kentucky to service the moonshine stills. Probably an April Fool's spoof. No real evidence.

68. June 1997. *Mountain Biker*. "The Search for the Cupertino Bikes," by Joel Smith. The story of Russ Mahon and the Cupertino mountain bikes.

69. 1999. *Fat Tire: A Celebration of the Mountain Bike*. By Amici Design. Includes a good general history of the mountain bike from its beginnings to 1999.

70. Charlie Kelly's website is a veritable treasure trove of historical mountain bike information. It's at *http://sonic.net/ ~ckelly/Seekay/mtbwelcome.htm*.

71. 2007. "Klunkerz: A Film About Mountain Biking" DVD. By Billy Savage. Published by Green Planet Films.

Index